SO YOU THINK YOU KNOW
JANE AUSTEN?

JANE AUSTEN was born in 1775 in the village of Steventon, Hampshire, the daughter of an Anglican clergyman. The Austens were cultured but not at all rich, though one of Austen's brothers was adopted by a wealthy relative. Other brothers followed professional careers in the church, the navy, and banking. With the exception of one brief period away at school, Austen and her elder sister Cassandra, her closest friend and confidante, were educated at home. Austen's earliest surviving work, written at Steventon whilst still in her teens, is dedicated to her family and close female friends. Between 1801 and 1809, her least productive period, Austen lived in Bath, where her father died in 1805, and in Southampton. In 1809, she moved with her mother, Cassandra, and their great friend Martha Lloyd to Chawton, Hampshire, her home until her death at Winchester in 1817. During this time, Austen published four of her major novels: *Sense and Sensibility* (1811); *Pride and Prejudice* (1813); *Mansfield Park* (1814); and *Emma* (1816), visiting London regularly to oversee their publication. *Persuasion* and *Northanger Abbey* were published posthumously in 1818.

JOHN SUTHERLAND is Emeritus Professor of Modern English Literature at University College London, and is the author of many books, most recently *Stephen Spender: The Authorized Biography* (2004). He has also edited *Vanity Fair*, *The Woman in White*, *The Way We Live Now*, and *Eminent Victorians* and has written *Is Heathcliff a Murderer?*, *Can Jane Eyre Be Happy?*, *Who Betrays Elizabeth Bennet?*, and (with Cedric Watts) *Henry V, War Criminal?* for Oxford World's Classics. He writes a regular column for the *Guardian*, and reviews for a number of journals as well as on radio.

DEIRDRE LE FAYE is a renowned Austenian scholar, and the editor of *Jane Austen's Letters* (1995). Her other works include *The Jane Austen Cookbook* (1995), *Writers' Lives: Jane Austen* (1998), *Jane Austen: The World of Her Novels* (2002), *Jane Austen's 'Outlandish Cousin': The Life and Letters of Eliza De Feuillide* (2002), *Jane Austen: A Family Record* (1989; new edition 2004) ~~ ~ articles in scholarly journals.

OXFORD WORLD'S CLASSICS

*For over 100 years Oxford World's Classics have brought
readers closer to the world's great literature. Now with over 700
titles—from the 4,000-year-old myths of Mesopotamia to the
twentieth century's greatest novels—the series makes available
lesser-known as well as celebrated writing.*

*The pocket-sized hardbacks of the early years contained
introductions by Virginia Woolf, T. S. Eliot, Graham Greene,
and other literary figures which enriched the experience of reading.
Today the series is recognized for its fine scholarship and
reliability in texts that span world literature, drama and poetry,
religion, philosophy and politics. Each edition includes perceptive
commentary and essential background information to meet the
changing needs of readers.*

OXFORD WORLD'S CLASSICS

JOHN SUTHERLAND AND
DEIRDRE LE FAYE

So You Think You Know Jane Austen?

A Literary Quizbook

OXFORD
UNIVERSITY PRESS

OXFORD
UNIVERSITY PRESS

Great Clarendon Street, Oxford OX2 6DP

Oxford University Press is a department of the University of Oxford.
It furthers the University's objective of excellence in research, scholarship,
and education by publishing worldwide in

Oxford New York

Auckland Cape Town Dar es Salaam Hong Kong Karachi Kuala Lumpur
Madrid Melbourne Mexico City Nairobi New Delhi Shanghai Taipei Toronto

With offices in

Argentina Austria Brazil Chile Czech Republic France Greece
Guatemala Hungary Italy Japan South Korea Poland Portugal
Singapore Switzerland Thailand Turkey Ukraine Vietnam

Oxford is a registered trade mark of Oxford University Press
in the UK and in certain other countries

Published in the United States
by Oxford University Press Inc., New York

First published as an Oxford World's Classics paperback 2005
Reissued 2009

British Library Cataloguing in Publication Data

Data available

Library of Congress Cataloging in Publication Data

Data available

ISBN 978-0-19-953899-7

Typeset in Ehrhardt
by RefineCatch Limited, Bungay, Suffolk
Printed in Great Britain by
Clays Ltd, Elcograf S.p.A.

The manufacturer's authorised representative in the EU for product safety is
Oxford University Press España S.A. of El Parque Empresarial San Fernando de Henares,
Avenida de Castilla, 2 – 28830 Madrid (www.oup.es/en or product.safety@oup.com
OUP España S.A. also acts as importer into Spain of products made by the manufacturer.

CONTENTS

CONTENTS

INTRODUCTION

FOR most of the last century, Oxford University Press was the self-appointed custodian of the reputation of Jane Austen—a reputation which had some notable fluctuations before she became established as one of the two or three greatest novelists our literature has produced. R. W. Chapman's five-volume edition of the major fiction established a new standard of textual accuracy and discreet annotation when it first came out in 1923. Over the following decades Chapman edited and published the author's letters, her 'minor works', and those family materials that have formed the nucleus of all subsequent biographies of Austen. In the mid-1960s Chapman's edition was re-edited as *The Oxford Illustrated Jane Austen* by Mary Lascelles and Brian Southam (in six volumes). In 1995 OUP published Deirdre Le Faye's new and enlarged edition of Austen's letters.

For the general reader, OUP produced its handsome hardback 'World's Classics' editions which supplied generations of Janeites until the 1950s. Three decades later the paperback, annotated World's Classics (now Oxford World's Classics) editions of the novels were launched.

This small book will occupy a small corner in OUP's Austen library. It is derived from a teaching method which can conveniently be called 'Quiz and Questionnaire'. Essentially, it means approaching the text of a novel from two directions. The first assesses what one, as reader, knows factually (for example, 'how old is Catherine Morland when she makes her first entrance at the Upper Rooms at Bath?'). How well do you know, or remember, the narrative? The quiz will tell.

The second approach tests what one knows—or can plausibly construct—by deduction and hypothesis ('Has Catherine ever been to London?'). I have added to the mixture a few queries and quibbles and some interpretative problems. How deep can you get into the novel? Can you 'feel', seismographically, what is happening in the background of the novel, but not narrated? (Surely

Henry must know that the Morlands are not rich, and that his father is fooling himself?)

The pay-off from applying this two-pronged method to fiction like Jane Austen's is that she loads her stories with what Henry James called 'solidity of specification'. Real-world questions can legitimately be asked of realistic fiction. The advantage of Q & Q is, the authors contend, twofold: it is a pleasing way to read and, whatever its critical simple-mindedness, it brings the reader close to the text.

This book is primarily concerned with what can be discovered in the texts of the six novels, carefully read. Ideally, the reader should have at hand (in addition, of course, to the OWC annotated editions) Deirdre Le Faye's *Jane Austen: The World of Her Novels* (2002) which reconstructs the social and historical context to these richest of works.

So You Think You Know Jane Austen? originated in the pleasure which the authors take in the novels and their hope is that, in a small way, this challenge to reading expertise will enhance the pleasure that other readers take in *Northanger Abbey*, *Sense and Sensibility*, *Pride and Prejudice*, *Emma*, *Mansfield Park*, and *Persuasion*. Would that the list were longer.

JOHN SUTHERLAND

THE QUIZZES

A Note on the Quizzes

The quizzes and questions are arranged in four levels, of ascending difficulty. The first ('**Level One: Brass Tacks**') contains straightforwardly factual questions which admit of direct, unequivocal answers. The second test ('**Level Two: Factual but Tricky**') contains a more demanding set of questions of basically the same kind. The next test ('**Level Three: Very Tricky—and Occasionally Deductive**') approaches mastermind difficulty in terms of factual reference and involves some interpretative deduction as well. The Fourth Test ('**Level Four: The Interpretative Zone**') invites deduction and speculation.

The answers, following the italicized questions, will be found at the end of the book.

Sense and Sensibility

Introductory Note on the Novel

Sense and Sensibility was the first published of Jane Austen's novels. Composition was begun perhaps as early as 1795 (some authorities suggest a year or two later). What is certain is that the novel was published in November 1811, on commission (that is, the author paying for the production costs, in return for a larger share of profit) by the London publisher Thomas Egerton. Austen began negotiations with Egerton (with her brother Henry as her intermediary) in 1810. While the manuscript was still in her hands, she made some updating references (to Scott's being a popular poet, for example). The first edition of *Sense and Sensibility* was obviously successful, a second edition appearing in November 1813.

Much may have happened between the novel's conception, composition, and belated publication. No manuscript and little other primary evidence remains. It was begun as an epistolary work (that is, a novel narrated in letters), originally entitled 'Elinor and Marianne', and read to the Austen family in 1795. It was reorganized as a third-person narrative (with Elinor as principal centre of consciousness and Austen's narrative voice) probably in 1797. The work was then in hand for more than a decade – at which point Austen already had *Pride and Prejudice* ready for publication.

It is significant that Jane Austen was 19 (Elinor's age, and the age at which Marianne marries) when she began to write the story. The author, that is to say, was herself passing through the years which are at the centre of the narrative.

It is not easy to locate the exact historical time period of *Sense and Sensibility*. Is it a 1790s novel, or a Regency novel? There is, even by Austen's standards, an absence of helpful historical markers. None the less, the balance of evidence seems to point to the 1790s rather than the Regency. The references, for example, to Marianne's curls being 'all tumbled down her back', and 'the pin in her ladyship's head dress' scratching little Annamaria when Lady Middleton cuddles her—recall hairstyles of the earlier period. Ten or fifteen years later, Lady Middleton would have been wearing a cap, not a head-dress; and it is likely that Marianne's curls would have been lifted up into a ponytail style, rather than falling down loose. A reference in passing to a needlebook 'made by emigrants' also implies the 1790s.

Level One: Brass Tacks

1/1 Under what circumstances did the Henry Dashwood family move in with Henry's uncle, old Mr Dashwood?

1/2 How much money do the Dashwood women have between them, and how much do each of the three daughters individually possess?

1/3 How much does the Norland estate yield annually to its new owner, Mr John Dashwood?

1/4 Mr John Dashwood's first intention was to honour his father's deathbed wish by giving his half-sisters £3,000. How much, after being persuaded by his mercenary wife on the matter, does he finally resolve to give them? And how much does he actually come across with?

1/5 What is the largest and most cumbersome object the Dashwood ladies have to transport to Barton Cottage?

1/6 In which month of the year do the Dashwood ladies arrive at Barton Park?

1/7 What is Sir John's favourite term for handsome young girls (for whom he clearly has an eye)?

1/8 Mrs Jennings is a widow with 'an ample jointure'. What is that?

1/9 What is Willoughby, a Somersetshire man, doing in Devon?

1/10 What word sums up Lady Middleton?

1/11 Where do the Miss Careys live?

1/12 What time of day (according to Sir John Middleton) does Willoughby usually rise in the morning?

1/13 Who, apart from Marianne, is Willoughby's 'inseparable companion' at Barton Cottage?

1/14 Where does Edward Ferrars stay when he comes to Devon and where does his horse stay?

1/15 Mrs Ferrars has been trying to push Edward into taking up a profession. What has she suggested, what are his objections, and what does he eventually do, at the end of the novel?

1/16 What is the epithet most accurately applied to Charlotte Palmer?

1/17 Who (before Elinor is spitefully told) is the only other person who knows about the secret engagement of Lucy and Edward?

1/18 How much does the public postal service, for a letter, cost in the world of *Sense and Sensibility*?

1/19 What is Mrs Jennings's 'favourite meal'?

1/20 What is given Marianne to relieve her 'hysteria', in the extremity of her disappointed love?

1/21 Whom does Mrs Ferrars intend her son, Edward, to marry, and how much is the young lady worth?

1/22 Who is the taller child, William Middleton or Harry Dashwood?

1/23 How, when she visits him at Cleveland, does Elinor find Mr Thomas Palmer changed?

1/24 What are Willoughby's last words to Elinor?

1/25 What is the only fly in the ointment for Edward and Elinor in the vicarage at Delaford?

☞ *Check answers at the back of the volume. If you scored over 15 proceed to Level Two ('Factual but Tricky'). If you scored over 10 but under 15, skim the novel again. Over 5 but under 10, reread the novel. Under 5, throw this book away and watch TV.*

Level Two: Factual but Tricky

2/1 The first sentences of Miss Austen's novels are famously memorable ('It is a truth universally acknowledged', etc.). Can you remember that with which *Sense and Sensibility* opens?

2/2 What may we assume old Mr Dashwood's (he who dies, at an advanced age, on the first page) first name to be?

2/3 Who educated Elinor and Marianne?

2/4 What qualities does Edward Ferrars possess?

2/5 What was Colonel Brandon an officer in?

2/6 What do we know of Mrs Smith?

2/7 What was Willoughby doing, walking up the High-Church Down?

2/8 Is Willoughby's scooping the fallen Marianne up into his arms at her request?

2/9 Who is Marianne walking with, when she has her momentous fall?

2/10 In what way, before she knows the older woman, does Elinor think Lady Middleton is to be preferred over her mother?

2/11 What is the play of Shakespeare's that the Dashwoods were reading during evenings at Barton Cottage with Willoughby, and never completed?

2/12 Who says 'these bottoms must be dirty in winter' and what does the statement mean?

2/13 What gift does the sycophantic Lucy make for little Annamaria Middleton?

2/14 Why is Marianne so keen for cold weather to arrive in London?

2/15 Why does Mrs Jennings not attend the ball at which Willoughby so cruelly humiliates Marianne?

2/16 Who says 'And what good does talking ever do'?

2/17 Do we ever know Colonel Brandon's Christian name?

2/18 Where do the Miss Steeles stay when in London?

2/19 Who says of whom: 'At her time of life, any thing of an illness destroys the bloom for ever! Her's has been such a very short one!'

2/20 What is Mrs John Dashwood's reaction on learning that her brother Edward is secretly engaged to Lucy Steele?

2/21 Overhearing part of Elinor's conversation with Colonel Brandon about Edward's marriage, Mrs Jennings misunderstands who is to marry whom, and says later 'Mr Ferrars is to be the man'; what does she mean?

2/22 When Elinor makes her delayed visit, after a week, to the John Dashwood household in Harley Street, she is 'denied'. What does this mean?

2/23 When Marianne thinks the end has come what is her dying wish?

2/24 What is Edward's 'simple' errand on his second visit to Barton Cottage?

2/25 Which of the sisters is a mother at the end of the novel?

☞ *Answers at the back of the book. Anything over 12 is good,*
indicating either strong memory or recent acquaintance.
Go on to Level Three ('Very Tricky—and Occasionally
Deductive') which requires, in addition to intimate know-
ledge of the text, an ability to make plausible deductions
from it.

Level Three: Very Tricky—and Occasionally Deductive

3/1 Where does Elinor's good sense come from? No one else in her immediate family seems to possess it.

3/2 Why are Mrs Henry Dashwood and her daughters not on closer terms with the John Dashwood family?

3/3 Fanny Dashwood 'had never been a favourite with any of her husband's family'. Why not?

3/4 What does Mr Henry Dashwood say to his son, John, as he (Henry) is dying, about supporting his surviving women-folk?

3/5 What is Edward Ferrars doing in his six months' stay at Norland, while the Henry Dashwood ladies are still in the house?

3/6 Why does Sir John Middleton write to Mrs Henry Dashwood, out of the blue, inviting her to stay at Barton Cottage?

3/7 In what ways is Barton Cottage 'defective'?

3/8 How many bedrooms does Barton Cottage have, and what issues does this raise in the modern reader's mind?

3/9 Willoughby, when we first meet him, is accompanied by two pointers. One of them, a 'black bitch', recurs in the narrative (Sir John has a particular fancy for the animal). What is this favourite pointer's name?

3/10 What does it mean that Marianne's figure is 'not so correct as her sister's', and that she has very brown skin?

3/11 Some six mothers are portrayed at some length in *Sense and Sensibility*. Which of them can be seen as the best?

3/12 What is the name of the horse Willoughby intends to give Marianne, and what is the allusion in its name?

3/13 What, from Marianne's later utterances, may we deduce that Willoughby has told her about what life will be like at Allenham for the future Mrs Willoughby?

3/14 Mrs Henry Dashwood, as the relationship has (to her maternal eye) reached its crucial stage, is content that Willoughby and Marianne should be left alone—for what will surely be a proposal on his part. Normally, of course, they would be chaperoned. Is a proposal his intention?

3/15 No letter is expected by Marianne from Willoughby. Why not?

3/16 Why does Edward Ferrars start in alarm when Marianne says, without any ulterior meaning, that he is 'reserved'?

3/17 What colour is Elinor's hair?

3/18 What did the late Mr Jennings do by way of occupation?

3/19 Where has Charlotte Palmer been educated?

3/20 What kind of carriage does Charlotte Palmer have?

3/21 What is Marianne's characteristic expletive, when surprised?

3/22 How much wealth does Miss Grey, Willoughby's intended, have to give to her prospective lord and master?

3/23 How, as a special mark of favour, does Mrs John Dashwood address Lucy Steele?

3/24 How is Colonel Brandon's 'I am afraid it cannot take place very soon' understood by the eavesdropping Mrs Jennings, and how is it understood by Elinor, whom he is talking to in his calm voice?

3/25 What does Willoughby euphemistically call his seduction of Eliza, in describing it to Elinor?

☞ *Answers at the back of the book. The factual questions are very difficult, and some of the questions involve interpretation. If you score anything over 10, go forward to Level Four ('The Interpretative Zone'). If your deductive answers genuinely strike you as more convincing, or ingenious, than mine, give yourself a bonus point (or more).*

Level Four: The Interpretative Zone

4/1 How should we read the title? Is it 'Sense *versus* Sensibility'? Or is the conjunction the more neutral '*and*' as in 'Duck and Green Peas'? Which of the two heroines represents which moral quality and which is finally endorsed?

4/2 How old are the four Dashwood women at the start of the narrative, and what should we read into their respective ages?

4/3 Old Mr Dashwood's will creates the principal complication of the ensuing plot—leaving, as he does, only a life interest to his nephew Henry (whose subsequent life is sadly short). What, as best as one can reconstruct it, is the Dashwood family tree and line of inheritance it creates?

4/4 Why does Sir John charge Mrs Henry Dashwood rent, albeit an 'uncommonly moderate' rent?

4/5 Is Mrs Jennings's inveterate addiction to match-making 'vulgarity' and nothing more?

4/6 Deaths are significant moments in the world of *Sense and Sensibility*—the moment at which inheritances happen and riches are distributed. What do we deduce to be the life expectancy of wealth-holders in the class of genteel, idle, English people who inhabit the world of *Sense and Sensibility*?

4/7 What, apart from misadventure, may we deduce from Marianne's spraining her ankle?

4/8 Why is Colonel Brandon so concerned with the validity of 'second attachments'?

4/9 When, against her will, Marianne turns down Willoughby's offer of Queen Mab, she communicates the bad news to him in 'a low voice'. How can Elinor (as she does) overhear this conversation and the telling fact that Willoughby addresses her sister by her Christian name?

4/10 Austen does not directly relate what is said between Marianne and Willoughby in the meeting at which, everyone at Barton Cottage expects, he will propose. What, can we deduce, does he say about seeing Marianne in the future?

4/11 In what circumstances does the moral paragon Elinor think it proper to tell lies?

4/12 How long does the 23-year-old Lucy Steele claim to have been 'engaged' to Edward Ferrars, and should we believe her?

4/13 What demonstrates, in Lucy's interpretation of things, that they are indeed plighted?

4/14 What should we make of Mrs Jennings's comment 'Upon my word I never saw a young woman so desperately in love in my life! My girls were nothing to her, and yet they used to be foolish enough . . .'?

4/15 Colonel Brandon says (rather paradoxically) that Marianne and Willoughby 'openly correspond' (that is, exchange private letters). How does he know?

4/16 What, from the two hearts which he has won (Eliza's and Marianne's), do we deduce is Willoughby's principal taste in young women?

4/17 Where does Colonel Brandon learn of Willoughby's infamous conduct towards Marianne?

4/18 Who, do we learn, was Colonel Brandon's 'first attachment' and what can we gather about her?

4/19 Willoughby later says it is 'impossible' for him to marry Eliza Williams (junior). Why?

4/20 Does anyone get injured or killed in the duel between Willoughby and Brandon?

4/21 What is Elinor doing in Gray's in Sackville Street, and why is she doing it, when she unwittingly observes Robert Ferrars?

4/22 What is Robert Ferrars doing at the Sackville Street jewellers?

4/23 What does the incorrigibly mean Mrs John Dashwood give the Steele girls by way of personal gift?

4/24 Who tells Mrs John Dashwood that Lucy Steele is engaged to be married to her brother, Edward?

4/25 Why, if he thinks Lucy Steele the 'merest awkward country girl without style, or elegance', does Robert Ferrars go out of his way to call on her?

☞ *Check answers at the end of the book. Give yourself a bonus for every interpretative answer which seems to you (1) correct, or (2) more plausible, witty, or ingenious than that which I offer.*

Total all your marks. If you scored 100 (or more), write your own book. Over 60, congratulations; 30 or less—you will have the pleasure of rereading Sense and Sensibility.

Pride and Prejudice

Introductory Note on the Novel

Pride and Prejudice was written early (October 1796–August 1797) and published late, by Thomas Egerton (who paid £110 for the copyright, a price generated by the success of *Sense and Sensibility*) in January 1813. Initially entitled 'First Impressions', the text (a favourite with the Austen family) was probably revised (or as the author put it, 'lop't and crop't') a couple of years before its eventual acceptance. There are few historical markers in the text, but the narrative is probably set around the 1790s period of the initial composition. One of the principal markers is the billeting of militia troops in the Meryton area, among the civilian population. This practice ceased after 1795, with the construction of military barracks for such forces. Contemporary readers would probably have apprehended that the action of the novel was, therefore, antedated to an earlier wartime period.

Level One: Brass Tacks

1/1 Describe, with their Austenish epithet (or characteristic mark), the five Bennet girls, in order of age.

1/2 What does Mr Bingley wear on his first visit to the Bennets at Longbourn?

1/3 How many sisters does Mr Bingley have?

1/4 What is Mr Bennet's estate, Longbourn, worth, and who will eventually inherit it?

1/5 How old is Charlotte Lucas?

1/6 What first begins to attract Darcy to Elizabeth?

1/7 Who is the commanding officer of the militia regiment which has been posted in Meryton for the winter, and who is the regiment's second in command?

1/8 Where do the Bennet girls get their reading matter?

1/9 What relation is Mr Philips to Elizabeth, and what is his profession?

1/10 Who introduces Wickham to the Bennet young ladies, and what do we know of him?

1/11 How much did the chimney-piece in Lady Catherine's drawing-room cost?

1/12 How much does Wickham estimate that Pemberley is worth?

1/13 How much money does Mr Collins lose at whist?

1/14 What is Sir William's favourite epithet?

1/15 What are Mary's shortcomings as a singer and pianist?

1/16 What does Mrs Gardiner inform her sister-in-law is the latest style in fashionable London?

1/17 To whom does the faithless Wickham transfer his affections, and why?

1/18 How old is Elizabeth?

1/19 How far is it from Longbourn to Hunsford?

1/20 What is George Wickham's relationship to Fitzwilliam Darcy?

1/21 How old is Darcy?

1/22 Why cannot Lydia buy lunch for Elizabeth and Jane, when she meets them at an inn on their return from London?

1/23 Where does the ——shire militia go in the second week in May, after wintering at Meryton?

1/24 Why does Jane have to cede her place to Lydia, six years her junior?

1/25 Why does Mr Bennet advise Mr Collins to 'stand by the nephew'?

☞ *Check answers at the back of the volume. If you scored over 15, proceed to Level Two ('Factual but Tricky'). If you scored over 10 but under 15, skim the novel again. Over 5 but under 10, reread the novel. Under 5, throw this book away and watch TV.*

Level Two: Factual but Tricky

2/1 Lizzy is described as 'trimming a hat'. What does this indicate?

2/2 How has Sir William Lucas enriched and ennobled himself?

2/3 What card-game do Jane and Bingley find they prefer?

2/4 Why does Elizabeth not play loo with the Bingley sisters?

2/5 Why is Miss Bingley so very keen to mend Darcy's pen, as he is writing a letter to his sister?

2/6 What news do Lydia and Kitty bring Jane and Lizzy from Meryton, when the older sisters return from visiting Netherfield?

2/7 How long has Mr Collins been ordained, when he writes to Mr Bennet on 15 October?

2/8 How old is Georgiana Darcy?

2/9 What is the connection of Lady Catherine de Bourgh and Lady Anne Darcy (deceased)?

2/10 How much money do we learn (from Mr Collins, who has taken care to find out) Elizabeth will bring to her marriage? And how much will Charlotte bring?

2/11 Why, as the narrator uncompromisingly informs us, does Charlotte accept Mr Collins, and what is Elizabeth's one-word expletive on hearing that (three days after proposing to her, Miss Bennet) he has offered himself to Miss Lucas?

2/12 Why does Mr Gardiner, Mrs Bennet's brother, come to Longbourn and what do we learn of him?

2/13 What is Mrs Gardiner's connection with Pemberley?

2/14 What is Mr Collins's favourite recreation?

2/15 Is Rosings a venerable old building?

2/16 When Lady Catherine asks, 'Are any of your younger sisters out, Miss Bennet?', what does the old battleaxe mean?

2/17 Why cannot Colonel Fitzwilliam propose to Elizabeth?

2/18 Why does Elizabeth spend six weeks at Hunsford?

2/19 When is Lydia's birthday?

2/20 What is the original purpose of Elizabeth's journey north with the Gardiners?

2/21 What bond forges an immediate friendship between the aristocratic Darcy and the mercantile Mr Gardiner?

2/22 Who is said to have 'tolerable' teeth, and by whom?

2/23 What is Mr Bennet's response, on learning of Wickham's elopement with his daughter?

2/24 What is 'peculiar' in the engagement of Anne de Bourgh to Fitzwilliam Darcy?

2/25 Which of the Bennet sisters is destined to stay at home, unmarried, and care for her parents?

☞ *Answers at the back of the book. Anything over 12 is good, indicating either strong memory or recent acquaintance. Go on to Level Three ('Very Tricky—and Occasionally Deductive') which requires, in addition to intimate knowledge of the text, an ability to make plausible deductions from it.*

Level Three: Very Tricky—and
Occasionally Deductive

3/1 Who informs Mrs Bennet that Netherfield Park is to be let, and what more do we learn of the lady subsequently in the narrative?

3/2 What should we read into the fact that Lydia is both the youngest and the tallest of the Bennet girls?

3/3 Why is Lizzy Mr Bennet's favourite and Mary his least favourite daughter?

3/4 What is Mrs Bennet's characteristic indisposition, and what do we deduce from it?

3/5 Why has Mr Bingley, who has been living in London, chosen to take a house in rural Hertfordshire?

3/6 How much annual income does Longbourn credit the eligible Mr Bingley with having, and where does it come from?

3/7 Why does Miss Bingley so abuse Elizabeth (about her dirty petticoat and 'country' manners, and so on)?

3/8 What are the implications of Darcy's remark, 'I cannot comprehend the neglect of a family library in such days as these'?

3/9 Where, cattily, does Miss Bingley suggest that the portrait of his future 'uncle and aunt Philips' (country attorney and his wife) be placed at Pemberley?

3/10 Why has Mr Collins offered his 'olive branch' to Mr Bennet?

3/11 What profession was Wickham first destined for, and what do we know of his back story?

3/12 What fault of good manners does Mr Collins display, in introducing himself (with welcome bulletins about Lady Catherine's health) to Darcy, and how does he justify the breach?

3/13 Why does Elizabeth take such a tender interest in Jane's marriage affairs, and so little in those of her younger sisters?

3/14 Why does Lady Catherine disapprove of entails?

3/15 What does Darcy mean by his remark to Elizabeth (which 'surprises' her), '*You* cannot have been always at Longbourn'?

3/16 Where and when (and how) did Wickham make his attempt on Georgiana?

3/17 What do we know of Mary King?

3/18 What may we read into the university background of some of the novel's main characters?

3/19 What characterizes Lydia's letters to Kitty, from Brighton?

3/20 What is the sagacious Mary's response, on learning of Lydia's running away?

3/21 Why does Wickham accept the surprisingly modest settlement of £100 p.a. from Mr Bennet?

3/22 Where does Wickham (with Darcy's money) get his commission in the 'regulars'?

3/23 How does Elizabeth learn that Darcy was at the wedding of Lydia and Wickham?

3/24 Does Lydia know about the financial assistance which Darcy has made? Is she, that is to say, an accomplice in this extortion?

3/25 Why does Mrs Bennet assume that Elizabeth and Darcy will be married by 'special licence'?

☞ *Answers at the back of the book. The factual questions are very difficult, and some of the questions involve interpretation. If you score anything over 10, go forward to Level Four ('The Interpretative Zone'). If your deductive answers genuinely strike you as more convincing, or ingenious, than mine, give yourself a bonus point (or more).*

Level Four: The Interpretative Zone

4/1 How long have Mr and Mrs Bennet been married (an easy question), and why on earth did he marry her (the most difficult question in the novel)?

4/2 What can we reconstruct of Mr and Mrs Bennet's 'back story'?

4/3 Why does Mr Bennet tease and tantalize his wife so?

4/4 When, at the Meryton ball that brings the principals together, Darcy makes his disagreeable remark that 'She is tolerable; but not handsome enough to tempt *me*; and I am in no humour at present to give consequence to young ladies who are slighted by other men', he is overheard by Elizabeth (and, as we apprehend, her mother). Does he mean to be overheard? Should we perhaps assume the music momentarily stopped? Is he, perhaps, a little deaf?

4/5 In conversation with Charlotte (who was at the Meryton ball), an exasperated Elizabeth says that Jane 'danced four dances with [Bingley]'. As the eagle-eyed Mrs Bennet notes (frequently), it was two dances only. What do we read into the error?

4/6 Why does Darcy, at the Netherfield ball, resolve to break up the romance between Bingley and Jane?

4/7 Why does Mr Collins ask Mrs Bennet's permission to propose to Elizabeth, but not Mr Bennet's? And why, three days later, does he propose to Charlotte without consulting either of the young lady's parents?

4/8 Why does not Mr Bennet encourage his heir, Mr Collins, in his addresses to his eligible daughters? If not Lizzy (whom he does not want to lose) then Mary?

4/9 Who does Darcy bring to Rosings with him, and what plot details may we weave around it?

4/10 When Darcy lists as the disqualifications of Elizabeth's family the 'want of propriety' of her mother and younger sisters and 'occasionally . . . your father', what is he thinking of?

4/11 How many professions and occupations has Wickham had?

4/12 What are the salient features of Pemberley that so delight the judicious Elizabeth Bennet?

4/13 Why *does* Wickham elope with Lydia?

4/14 Why, at Pemberley, does Elizabeth confide Lydia's elopement to Darcy?

4/15 How does Mr Collins learn of the elopement, and what does he do with his information?

4/16 What can we deduce about Wickham's conduct during his three months at Brighton, leading up to the elopement?

4/17 Why, after he has married Lydia, is Elizabeth so friendly and amicable with Wickham?

4/18 In their post-proposal intimate conversations, Bingley tells Jane (who tells Elizabeth) 'that he was totally ignorant of my being in town last spring'. Is this plausible?

4/19 Who gave Lady Catherine de Bourgh the 'report of an alarming nature', that not only was Jane to marry Bingley, but that 'Miss Elizabeth Bennet, would, in all likelihood, be soon afterwards united to my own nephew, Mr Darcy'?

4/20 Lady Catherine de Bourgh boasts to Elizabeth that her daughter and Darcy are descended 'on the maternal side, from the same noble line; and, on the father's, from respectable, and ancient, though untitled families.' With the other information that Darcy's cousin Colonel Fitzwilliam is the son of an earl, what kind of family tree can one construct from this?

4/21 It is conventionally observed that Miss Austen never shows two gentlemen in conversation together without a lady present. Is there any exception to this rule of her fictional universe?

4/22 When, Jane asks Elizabeth, did Elizabeth begin to love Darcy? Elizabeth replies: 'I believe it must date from my first seeing his beautiful grounds at Pemberley.' Is this ironic, or is she really as affected by real estate as the remark might imply?

4/23 Mr Bennet says, some weeks after Lydia's wedding and on learning that Darcy had paid over the necessary bribes: 'And so Darcy did everything . . . Had it been your uncle's [Gardiner's] doing, I must and *would* have paid him.' Would he?

4/24 Why is the proud, cultivated and snobbish Darcy the 'inseparable' friend of Bingley, a man of limited intelligence and no firmness of mind?

4/25 Why does Bingley (and his future wife) so readily forgive Darcy for keeping from him, the previous winter, the fact that Jane was in London—causing huge pain to the lady?

☞ *Check answers at the end of the book. Give yourself a bonus for every interpretative answer which seems to you (1) correct (2) more plausible, witty, or ingenious than that which I offer.*

Total all your marks. If you scored 100 (or more), write your own book. Over 60, congratulations; 30 or less—you will have the pleasure of rereading Pride and Prejudice.

Northanger Abbey

Introductory Note on the Novel

Northanger Abbey is reckoned to be the third written of Austen's six major novels—although it was the last published, in a bundled, posthumous four-volume set with *Persuasion*. The circumstances of its early composition and belated publication are given in James Edward Austen-Leigh's *Memoir*, the 'Advertisement' to the December 1817 first edition, and some surviving letters. It seems that Austen completed the novel in 1798/9 (aged 24). The novel was sold to the bookseller, Crosby & Co., for £10, in 1803 (he was not, as legend has it, based in Bath, but London). It was promptly advertised as 'In the Press' (as 'Susan'). But by 1809, no novel had appeared. Nor, apparently, was any explanation given to the frustrated author. When Austen (under incognito) complained, Crosby offered to sell back the property for what he had given. Austen did not, apparently, recover the copyright until 1816 (Crosby not realizing that he had a manuscript by the author of *Pride and Prejudice*). Austen had a spare copy of the manuscript and may, over the years, have made other changes to 'Susan' than the title. But the consensus of scholarly opinion is that the novel is substantially what she wrote in 1798/9. The author died in July 1817 and *Northanger Abbey* was published, posthumously, by John Murray, six months later.

What reason can Crosby have had for keeping this vivacious work unread? It is suggested that he felt that its satire might dampen the inflamed demand for the 'Gothics' he specialized in. This, one speculates, is the only occasion in literary history in which the demure Miss Austen suffered censorship. For her wit, appropriately enough.

In the 'Advertisement by the Authoress' to Murray's edition, Austen notes that during its thirteen years in limbo 'places, manners, books, and opinions have undergone considerable changes'. Historically, the period between the Revolutionary Terror of 1789 and Waterloo changed the world utterly. Ingenious readers may find seismic tremors in the narrative. There is no clear reflection. One thing that did change (other than the fluctuating fashions of nubile maidens in the country's watering places) was England's roads. With the arrival of John McAdam and his new surfaces, 'gentleman coachmen' like John Thorpe might well have achieved the dizzy speeds in his gig that he unconvincingly boasts of ('look at his loins; only see how he moves; that horse *cannot* go less than ten miles an hour').

Level One: Brass Tacks

1/1 What is Mr Morland's profession? How well off is he? What is the source of his wealth?

1/2 How many children do the Reverend Mr and Mrs Morland have? How many of their Christian names do we know?

1/3 What boisterous games does Catherine play as a girl?

1/4 How many children do the rich Allens have?

1/5 How much money does Mr Morland give Catherine as her Bath allowance? What do we learn that she spends it on?

1/6 How old is Henry Tilney?

1/7 What is Henry's profession, and how does Catherine learn of it?

1/8 How much older than Catherine is 'Miss Thorpe' (that is, Isabella)?

1/9 What is the first, and what the second, novel Catherine and Isabella read together?

1/10 How much did John Thorpe pay Freeman, of Christ Church, for his gig?

1/11 Where are James and John students?

1/12 In Bath, after the Thursday evening ball, Catherine is exultant: 'her spirits danced within her, as she danced in her chair all the way home.' What chair is this?

1/13 What is Miss Tilney's first name?

1/14 What aspect of Catherine's walk does General Tilney particularly admire?

1/15 Where did Henry go to university?

1/16 What is Isabella Thorpe's family nickname?

1/17 What profession is James intended for?

1/18 In what service is Frederick Tilney a captain?

1/19 Is Captain Frederick the elder, or younger brother?

1/20 What was Northanger Abbey originally?

1/21 What does Catherine realize she has found in the black cabinet?

1/22 Does Henry have a butler at Woodston?

1/23 What are the 'friends of Henry's solitude' at Woodston?

1/24 What pretext does the General give for throwing Catherine out of Northanger Abbey, with a bare eight hours' notice and no servant?

1/25 Who has disabused the General as to Catherine's prospects?

☞ *Check answers at the back of the volume. If you scored over 15 proceed to Level Two ('Factual but Tricky'). If you scored over 10 but under 15, skim the novel again. Over 5 but under 10, reread the novel. Under 5, throw this book away and watch TV.*

Level Two: Factual but Tricky

2/1 When, and why, does Catherine give up her tomboy pursuits?

2/2 Where is Catherine brought up? What do we know of the place?

2/3 What happy accident takes Catherine to Bath?

2/4 How do Mrs Allen and Mrs Thorpe recognize each other?

2/5 What do we know of Henry's complexion, and what does it mean?

2/6 What colour dress (as Mrs Allen's needle-sharp eye notes) does Miss Tilney 'always wear'?

2/7 How does John Thorpe come to have known General Tilney?

2/8 Who does John Thorpe take on the jaunt to Clifton, when Catherine obstinately refuses?

2/9 Who gave Catherine a lecture on fashion and when?

2/10 What is Catherine's first response on being invited to Northanger Abbey?

2/11 Who says, 'after all that romancers may say, there is no doing without money'?

2/12 For what does the General rebuke Frederick on the day the rest of the family leave Bath?

2/13 By what transportation does Catherine go from Bath to Northanger Abbey?

2/14 Where is Henry's house, and living? What kind of house is it?

2/15 Who has the gift of Woodston?

2/16 How long ago did Mrs Tilney die, and of what?

2/17 What, when she finally effects an entrance, does Catherine find in the 'mysterious apartment'?

2/18 Since Lady Fraser is not in the neighbourhood and a big dinner at Northanger is therefore out of the question, what does General Tilney suggest?

2/19 How long has Catherine been at Northanger Abbey when General Tilney goes on his fateful visit to London for a week?

2/20 Why has Catherine, even before the General's wrathful return, suggested that she should, perhaps, leave?

2/21 What are Catherine's first thoughts when Eleanor disturbs her in her bedroom on Saturday night, 'on such an errand! . . . Oh! How shall I tell you!'?

2/22 In what sort of vehicle does Catherine travel back to Fullerton?

2/23 How long is it before Henry appears at Fullerton to propose?

2/24 What finally makes the General agree to the marriage of Henry and Catherine, and how does he phrase his consent?

2/25 How long do the lovers have to wait for paternal consent?

☞ *Answers at the back of the book. Anything over 12 is good, indicating either strong memory or recent acquaintance. Go on to Level Three ('Very Tricky—and Occasionally Deductive') which requires, in addition to intimate knowledge of the text, an ability to make plausible deductions from it.*

Level Three: Very Tricky—and
Occasionally Deductive

3/1 We are told that Catherine's father was 'a very respectable man, though his name was Richard'. What do we make of the gibe against this harmless Christian name?

3/2 What is Mrs Morland's favourite novel?

3/3 On the journey to Bath, Mrs Allen fears she has left her clogs at an inn. Why would a rich woman, fanatic about her wardrobe, wear these?

3/4 When Mrs Thorpe boasts about her children, how does the childless Mrs Allen console herself?

3/5 What reasons does John Thorpe give for not bothering to read Fanny Burney's *Camilla*?

3/6 What over the course of the novel do we learn of the Thorpes? How many of them are there at Bath and how should we picture them?

3/7 Catherine is frustratingly prevented from joining the dance at the Upper Rooms because John Thorpe absents himself in the card room. What is he doing there?

3/8 Why, having just arrived at Bath (to arrange accommodation for himself and his father and sister) does Henry suddenly leave, and what should we deduce from his departure?

3/9 How much money did the late Mrs Tilney (née Drummond) bring with her on marriage to the General?

3/10 This is a quiz. What does the slangy word mean in 1798 at Bath—when, for example, John Thorpe says that his sisters and their partners are the 'four greatest quizzes in the room'?

3/11 Who is John Thorpe's hunting companion?

3/12 What do we know of the Skinners?

3/13 How does Mr Morland respond to James's surprising declaration that he is in love and intends to marry?

3/14 What do we deduce from General Tilney's being disappointed by the non-arrival of his 'friends' the Marquis of Longtown and General Courteney?

3/15 Why does Henry say that Captain Tilney 'must be his own master'?

3/16 On the trip to Northanger Abbey we are informed that Catherine has a 'new writing desk'. What may we deduce from it?

3/17 What is the first sound that awakes Catherine on the morning after the night of the storm?

3/18 What is Eleanor Tilney's favourite walk and why?

3/19 What does Catherine find when she enters Henry's room at Northanger Abbey?

3/20 Why does the General not go to bed at the same time as the young ladies?

3/21 Why does Catherine not, as she plans, steal out at midnight to investigate the 'mysterious apartments' in which, she is convinced, the General's poor wife is secretly incarcerated?

3/22 How long was General Tilney's wife sick, before she dies? And was all her family round her?

3/23 It is a week between James's letter from Oxford, announcing that it is all over with his engagement, and Isabella's letter from Bath (which the family are hurriedly leaving) intimating that it is all over between herself and Captain Tilney (who has, treacherously, transferred his affections to Charlotte Davis). What has happened in this interval?

3/24 Why is Henry not at Northanger Abbey when Catherine is summarily banished?

3/25 How much does Catherine bring to the marriage?

☞ *Answers at the back of the book. The factual questions are very difficult, and some of the questions involve interpretation. If you score anything over 10, go forward to Level Four ('The Interpretative Zone'). If your deductive answers genuinely strike you as more convincing, or ingenious, than mine, give yourself a bonus point (or more).*

Level Four: The Interpretative Zone

4/1 Who, educationally, are Catherine's teachers and what do they teach her?

4/2 It would forestall a lot of complication (and rob us of an entertaining novel) if Henry, at Bath, had made enquiries of Catherine's background, her family's financial circumstances, and her relationship to the Allens. Why does he omit to do this?

4/3 Catherine gets her copies of Mrs Radcliffe's terrifying tales from Isabella. Where does Isabella get them from?

4/4 What do we learn, in this novel, about the diverse reading habits of gentlemen and ladies in the 1790s?

4/5 How is it that Henry, a bachelor clergyman with countrified tastes, knows so much about muslin and women's dress (that is, the difference between five- and nine-shilling muslin, and that Catherine's sprigged muslin will not wash well, and will fray)?

4/6 Catherine's response on seeing James drive up with John Thorpe at Cheap Street is an uncharacteristic exclamation (and near profanity): 'Good Heaven! 'tis James!' Why is she so surprised?

4/7 Catherine first identifies Henry's sister to Isabella as the 'young lady with the white beads round her head'. What do we later learn about these beads?

4/8 As they drive, John Thorpe asks Catherine: 'Old Allen is as rich as a Jew, is not he?' Later in the novel, he will make the same point about General Tilney being 'rich as a Jew'. What should we read into this apparent anti-Semitism?

4/9 When, at the Thursday assembly in the Pump Room, John Thorpe comes up to Catherine and says 'I thought you and I were to dance together', she says: 'you never asked me'. She knows, and so do we, that this is not true ('when he spoke to her [she] pretended not to hear him'). John (with some justice) calls it 'a cursed shabby trick'. Is it?

4/10 General Tilney, on his first inspection of Catherine, is described as 'a very handsome man, of a commanding aspect, past the bloom, but not past the vigour of life'. What do we know of his military career?

4/11 Does Catherine really not understand that John Thorpe is proposing marriage when he comes on her alone in Edgar's Buildings, before leaving for London?

4/12 Why does Henry seemingly acquiesce in his brother's campaign to seduce Isabella? What is he saying in the 'whispered conversation' that Catherine observes the brothers having, before Frederick embarks on his seduction of Isabella?

4/13 Catherine utters what looks like her second untruth when she tells Isabella that 'I did not see [John Thorpe] once that whole morning' when—as the reader will recall—the young man came to her alone, in Edgar's Buildings, to declare love and propose marriage (not something a young girl would readily forget). Catherine backtracks slightly by saying later, 'for the life of me, I cannot recollect it.' How should one react to this lapse of memory?

4/14 'What can your brother mean?', Catherine enquires of Henry, when his brother ostentatiously pays court to Isabella. What does Frederick mean?

4/15 What is the implication of Frederick's graceless farewell: 'How glad I shall be when you are all off'?

4/16 Why, female light-headedness apart, is Catherine so entranced with 'castles'?

4/17 Why does Jane Austen specifically tell us that Catherine has a 'charming game of play with a litter of puppies just able to roll about' in Henry's stable-yard at Woodston?

4/18 Why has the General put his sons into 'professions'? 'Employment', he says, is a good thing, even if one has private means. Why then does he have no employment, as far as we can make out?

4/19 In the company of Henry and Eleanor, General Tilney clearly seems to think that Catherine is the Allens' heiress (basing this on John Thorpe's misinformation). Are Eleanor and Henry similarly deceived as to Catherine's wealth and handsome prospects?

4/20 Why has Eleanor not yet married?

4/21 In his famous denunciation of Catherine's Gothic speculations, Henry talks of an England 'where every man is surrounded by a neighbourhood of voluntary spies, and where roads and newspapers lay every thing open'. What, historically, is he thinking of?

4/22 Why, given her preposterous and highly offensive conjectures, does Henry continue to 'indulge' Catherine, showing her, as we are told, 'rather more attention than usual'?

4/23 Catherine thinks Isabella is now engaged to Captain Tilney and that the Captain will gallop back to his father (as James rushed back to Fullerton) for paternal permission. Henry's guess is that his brother's marrying Isabella is 'not probable'. Has he known this from the first?

4/24 Catherine, on receiving the letter from Isabella describing Captain Tilney's desertion, poses a pertinent question: 'I do not understand what Captain Tilney has been about all this time. Why should he pay such attentions as to make quarrel with my brother, and then fly off himself?' Why?

4/25 Does Eleanor really not know why her father is so 'discomposed' and so furious with Catherine?

☞ *Check answers at the end of the book. Give yourself a*
bonus for every interpretative answer which seems to you
(1) correct (2) more plausible, witty, or ingenious than
that which I offer.

Total all your marks. If you scored 100 (or more), write
your own book. Over 60, congratulations; 30 or less—you
will have the pleasure of rereading **Northanger Abbey.**

Mansfield Park

Introductory Note on the Novel

Mansfield Park is the first of Jane Austen's three later novels,
written after a fallow period of some six years. It can plausibly be
taken as the first product of her full artistic power. She probably
began writing it around 1811–12 and finished in 1813. It was
offered to the publisher Egerton in that year and published in
May 1814, in three volumes. A second edition was published by
John Murray, in 1816.

Level One: Brass Tacks

1/1 How many children do the Price family have, and what are their names and ages at the start of the novel's main narrative?

1/2 How recently has Mrs Norris seen her sister, Mrs Price, at the time of the novel's main action?

1/3 What argument does Mrs Norris adduce for the safety of introducing a girl into the Bertram family—specifically with regard to the two young sons of the family?

1/4 Where does Miss Lee teach her three charges (Maria, Julia, and—latterly—Fanny) and what happens to the school-room?

1/5 Who does Mrs Norris declare can help Fanny dress herself?

1/6 How much older are Julia and Maria than Fanny?

1/7 How often does Fanny see William in the nine years she spends at Mansfield Park, and how often other members of her family?

1/8 How much income does Mrs Norris have?

1/9 What advantageous physical attributes does Henry Crawford possess?

1/10 What does Dr Grant think to be 'an insipid fruit at the best'?

1/11 Why has Mary Crawford never ridden a horse, before coming to Mansfield (and appropriating Fanny's steed)?

1/12 Who sits alongside Henry on the 'barouche box' on the visit to Sotherton?

1/13 What are the 'curious pheasants'?

1/14 Why did Mrs Whitaker, the housekeeper at Sotherton, turn away two housemaids?

1/15 What is Fanny Price's favourite reading?

1/16 Who is driven from home by a green goose?

1/17 Where did Tom Bertram meet the Honourable John Yates?

1/18 Who divulges to Sir Thomas that private theatricals were in prospect?

1/19 Who says, pathetically, 'Every body gets made but me'?

1/20 What does William bring Fanny from Sicily?

1/21 What vessel is William posted to, after his promotion to lieutenant?

1/22 Who thinks the alphabet 'her greatest enemy'?

1/23 When she says 'what a difference a vowel makes', what vowel is Mary Crawford thinking of?

1/24 How much does Sir Thomas give Fanny on her departure for Portsmouth?

1/25 Where does Tom have the accident which precipitates the fever which leads, eventually, to his moral regeneration?

☞ *Check answers at the back of the volume. If you scored over 15, proceed to Level Two ('Factual but Tricky'). If you scored over 10 but under 15, skim the novel again. Over 5 but under 10, reread the novel. Under 5, throw this book away and watch TV.*

Level Two: Factual but Tricky

2/1 We are told that Lieutenant Price's profession is such as 'no interest' (specifically Sir Thomas Bertram's) could reach. Is this true?

2/2 Why is Mrs Norris, the incarnation of selfishness, so keen that Fanny Price be brought to Mansfield Park?

2/3 What can we read into the fact that Mrs Price has nine children (and more pregnancies), Lady Bertram has four children, and Mrs Norris none?

2/4 What is Fanny's principal physical attraction?

2/5 Why does Lady Bertram give up the family house in town?

2/6 Sir Thomas's comment that William, when he comes to Mansfield Park, 'must find his sister at sixteen in some respects too much like his sister at ten' induces bitter tears in Fanny. What does the remark mean?

2/7 What are the Crawfords worth, and why do they come to stay with the Grants at Mansfield Park?

2/8 How many kinds of horse-drawn vehicle are mentioned in the narrative?

2/9 Why is Mary so long in discovering (not until they find themselves in the chapel at Sotherton) that Edmund is destined for the Church?

2/10 Which couple takes a 'serpentine course' in the novel, and what are the implications of the phrase?

2/11 Why do we not admire Maria Bertram for squeezing through the spiked fence at Sotherton (something that Fanny, even if she were wanton enough to do it, has not the strength to accomplish)? How should we picture this fence?

2/12 Who gives whom a lesson on astronomy, and with what results?

2/13 What 'duties' do we presume bring Tom back before his father, in September?

2/14 Who 'rants'?

2/15 In helping Mr Rushworth learn his part, Fanny is said to attempt to make 'an artificial memory for him'. What does this mean?

2/16 When he sees Fanny again, after four years, what is the first feature in her appearance which strikes William?

2/17 Why cannot Fanny play an instrument—the piano (like her cousins) or the harp (like Mary)?

2/18 Why is Mrs Norris so obsessed with saving Sir Thomas money (in such matters as forbidding any fire in Fanny's East room)?

2/19 What Shakespeare play does Fanny read to Lady Bertram, and what is its significance?

2/20 Why does Fanny insist (justifying her rejection of Henry) that 'we have not one taste in common', when they have recently been concurring in their love of Shakespeare, both of them knowledgeably?

2/21 At what time of year is Fanny packed off to Portsmouth?

2/22 What is the principal cause of quarrel between Susan and Betsey and what is its cure?

2/23 Why is Henry 'not satisfied about Maddison'?

2/24 How would Fanny's father, as he protests, deal with the delinquent Maria Rushworth?

2/25 What is Lady Bertram's exclamation, when Fanny returns to a devastated Mansfield?

☞ *Answers at the back of the book. Anything over 12 is good, indicating either strong memory or recent acquaintance. Go on to Level Three ('Very Tricky—and Occasionally Deductive') which requires, in addition to intimate knowledge of the text, an ability to make plausible deductions from it.*

Level Three: Very Tricky—and Occasionally Deductive

3/1 What, with regard to family planning, should we read into the first words of the novel, 'About thirty years ago'?

3/2 When the juvenile Edmund sends his cousin William half a guinea 'under the seal' what does this indicate?

3/3 Why does Edmund not get the family living of Mansfield when his uncle Norris dies?

3/4 Why does the lively, young, beautiful, and intelligent Maria Bertram accept the stupid Mr Rushworth (that is, not worth a light, or 'rushlight')?

3/5 Why has Tom, as we are told, given Fanny a profusion of work-boxes and netting-boxes?

3/6 Who profits most from the aborted production of *Lovers' Vows* at Mansfield Park?

3/7 What is Fanny's 'favourite indulgence'?

3/8 What is the sole occasion in the novel in which we are told that Fanny (almost) feels hatred for another human being?

3/9 How much is Edmund's promised living at Thornton Lacey worth to him?

3/10 When Edmund tells Fanny that she and Mary are 'the two dearest objects I have on earth' is he aware that he is both raising and dashing her hopes?

3/11 What does Fanny have round her neck at her first ball?

3/12 When, towards the end of Fanny's first ball, William comes up to her 'for a moment to visit her and working away his partner's fan as if for life', what does this mean?

3/13 How many card-games are depicted as being played in the narrative, and what do they imply?

3/14 Why is Sir Thomas a self-confessed 'advocate for early marriages'?

3/15 When Henry Crawford makes his proposal to Fanny, he first requests permission of Sir Thomas to do so—she being only 18, and three years beneath the age of marrying without parental consent. Why does not Henry apply to Fanny's father, at Portsmouth?

3/16 Why does Fanny (in near destitution at Portsmouth) exclaim to herself about Edmund and Mary, 'He will marry her, and be poor and miserable' when Mary has a £20,000 fortune, Edmund has a living worth over £700 a year and they both have extremely rich, and favourably inclined, relatives?

3/17 Fanny, when given intelligence about her cousins' activities in London, is disposed to think that the city is 'very much at war with all respectable attachments'. Has she ever visited the capital?

3/18 How penurious are the Price family, in their Portsmouth habitation?

3/19 What godparents are identified in the narrative?

3/20 Why is Fanny so surprised when her father behaves in a gentlemanlike way on meeting Mr Crawford?

3/21 What do we deduce from the description that Sunday dresses the Price family 'in their cleanest skins and best attire'?

3/22 What finally disillusions Edmund about Mary?

3/23 What is the last expression which Edmund sees on Mary's face, before leaving her for ever?

3/24 Where ('another country') do we deduce that Mrs Norris and the 'unfortunate Maria' are consigned to?

3/25 What happy event crowns the conclusion of the novel?

☞ *Answers at the back of the book. The factual questions are very difficult, and some of the questions involve interpretation. If you score anything over 10, go forward to Level Four ('The Interpretative Zone'). If your deductive answers genuinely strike you as more convincing, or ingenious, than mine, give yourself a bonus point (or more).*

Level Four: The Interpretative Zone

4/1 Jane Austen gave a great deal of thought to titles (how different, for example, our sense of *Pride and Prejudice* would be were it 'First Impressions'). Why is this her sole topographical title—instead of calling it, say, *Fanny Price*?

4/2 What do we know of the Ward family, from which the three sisters central to the ur-plot originate?

4/3 What should the reader make of the repeated references in the novel to Fanny's being 'delicate and puny'?

4/4 What do Sir Thomas and Tom Bertram actually do in their year or so in the Antigua estates?

4/5 Cynically, Mary Crawford assumes that happy marriages do not exist. Which are the happiest in *Mansfield Park*?

4/6 There is current disagreement about whether Jane Austen would have picked up (or, horrible to think, have intended) the *double entendre* which strikes us so embarrassingly, in Mary Crawford's comment, 'Certainly, my home at my uncle's brought me acquainted with a circle of admirals. Of *Rears* and *Vices*, I saw enough. No, do not be suspecting me of a pun, I entreat'. Or two puns? Is this a reference to nautical homosexuality?

4/7 What is the objection to theatricals at Mansfield Park?

4/8 What part in *Lovers' Vows* is Fanny, twice, invited (commanded) to play, and would she have agreed?

4/9 Why is Sir Thomas so affectionate ('Why do not I see my little Fanny?') towards his niece when he returns from Antigua?

4/10 One of the most famous moments in the novel is that in which Fanny recalls asking her uncle 'about the slave trade last night'. The question was, as she further recalls, followed by 'a dead silence'. What, if pressed, would Sir Thomas have said?

4/11 How long have the Grants been in possession of the Parsonage before Fanny is invited into the house?

4/12 When Fanny exclaims, 'there is nobleness in the name of Edmund. It is a name of heroism and renown . . . and seems to breath the spirit of chivalry' what do we assume she has been reading?

4/13 What gratification does Henry Crawford admit to have derived from the theatricals at Mansfield Park, disastrous as they were for others?

4/14 We are told that Henry Crawford 'had once seen Fanny dance . . . but in fact he could not for the life of him recall what her dancing had been'. When was this?

4/15 Why does Henry Crawford (if it is a private resolution) tell his sister, Mary, that 'my plan is to make Fanny Price in love with me'?

4/16 When Edmund goes off to be ordained, and stays with the Owen family, Mary apprehends that his friend Mr Owen 'had sisters—He might find them attractive'. Why is she never jealous of Fanny?

4/17 Mary calls her brother's plan to make Fanny fall in love with him a 'wicked project'. How wicked? Does he intend seduction?

4/18 Admiral Crawford (like Miss Lee) is a felt, but never seen presence in the novel. He is roundly described as 'vicious'. Mary suspects that Henry's manners may have been 'hurt by the contagion of his'. Does the remark have any overtones?

4/19 As she leads the ball, Fanny thinks of her cousins, Julia and Maria, 'so often as she had heard them wish for a ball at home as the greatest of felicities'—a felicity evidently denied these beautiful and eligible young women. Why has Sir Thomas decided to throw a ball for Fanny?

4/20 Apropos of his 'improving' tendencies, Henry Crawford lightly says, 'I never do wrong without gaining by it'. Is this the final outcome for him in the novel?

4/21 'I am quite determined to marry Fanny Price,' says Henry. Why?

4/22 One of Sir Thomas's strongest arguments in his first conversation, persuading Fanny to accept Henry's proposal, is that she should think of the 'advantage to your family'. 'You think only of yourself', he accuses. Is his argument strong?

4/23 'As a by-stander,' Fanny tells Edmund when explaining her rejection of Henry's proposal, 'perhaps I saw more than you did'. Is this true?

4/24 Sir Thomas sees Fanny's removal to Portsmouth as 'medicinal'. William looks forward to it as a great thing for his parents and siblings: 'You will tell my mother how it all ought to be, and you will be so useful to Susan, and you will teach Betsey, and make the boys love and mind you. How right and comfortable it will all be!' But it isn't—at least for Fanny. Why not?

4/25 Mrs Norris's bitter reflection on the disastrous elopements of the Bertram sisters is: 'Had Fanny accepted Mr Crawford, this could not have happened.' Is she right in her recrimination against Fanny?

☞ *Check answers at the end of the book. Give yourself a bonus for every interpretative answer which seems to you (1) correct (2) more plausible, witty, or ingenious than that which I offer.*

Total all your marks. If you scored 100 (or more), write your own book. Over 60, congratulations; 30 or less—you will have the pleasure of rereading Mansfield Park.

Emma

Introductory Note on the Novel

Emma was written between January 1814 and March 1815. The setting of the narrative's action would appear to be recent: 1813–14. By this period, Austen was a known and successful writer. Like *Sense and Sensibility*, the work was published on commission by the distinguished house of John Murray. It was published ('by the author of *Pride and Prejudice*, etc.') in December 1815 (dated 1816 on the title page). The novel was dedicated to the Prince Regent, at the request of the Carlton House Librarian, the Revd James Stanier Clarke.

Level One: Brass Tacks

1/1 The first sentence of *Emma*—as of all Jane Austen's novels—is epigrammatic and memorable. The first epithet ascribed to Emma in it is 'handsome'. What is the overtone of the term?

1/2 How long has Isabella been married? Where does she live, and what do we deduce from these facts?

1/3 What game do Mr Woodhouse and Emma play of an evening, at Hartfield?

1/4 How old is Mr Knightley?

1/5 How old is Mr Elton?

1/6 How often does Frank see his father?

1/7 Who was the widowed Mrs Bates's husband?

1/8 How old is Harriet, what distinguishes her from the other forty pupils at Mrs Goddard's, and who are her parents?

1/9 What colour (precisely) are Emma's eyes?

1/10 How many children does Isabella have, and what are their names?

1/11 What do we deduce from the fact that, in twenty-one years, Emma has not met the Martin family?

1/12 Who did Miss Nash's sister marry (very advantageously)?

1/13 Who is the best whist player in Highbury?

1/14 How large a contingent of servants and cattle does it take to get the five-strong Woodhouse party three-quarters of a mile to Randalls, on Christmas Eve?

1/15 What piece of land separates Randalls from Hartfield?

1/16 How long is it since Jane Fairfax was in Highbury?

1/17 Who was Jane Fairfax's father?

1/18 How much money did Miss Campbell bring to her marriage, by way of dowry? And how much are the other eligible ladies in the novel worth?

1/19 What is Mr Elton's first name? And Mr Knightley's? And Mrs Weston's? And Mr Woodhouse's?

1/20 What does Mr Knightley do with his last stored apples of the year?

1/21 With whom did Augusta Hawkins principally reside at Bath?

1/22 What is the name of Mrs Elton's cook?

1/23 Who is whose caro sposo and who is whose caro sposa?

1/24 What is Mrs Weston doing when she breaks the news of Frank's duplicity to Emma?

1/25 How long has Mr Knightley been in love with Emma?

☞ *Check answers at the back of the volume. If you scored over 15, proceed to Level Two ('Factual but Tricky'). If you scored over 10 but under 15, skim the novel again. Over 5 but under 10, reread the novel. Under 5, throw this book away and watch TV.*

Level Two: Factual but Tricky

2/1 How long has Miss Taylor been in Mr Woodhouse's employ, before becoming Mrs Weston, and what can we deduce from it?

2/2 What does John Knightley do for a living?

2/3 Why did Mr Knightley not go to Miss Taylor's wedding (thinking well of her, as he obviously does)?

2/4 How long did Mr Weston court Miss Taylor, and when did Emma contrive to 'make the match'?

2/5 Why did Emma not attend Mrs Goddard's 'honest, old-fashioned boarding-school'?

2/6 What do we know of Robert Martin, his practice as a farmer, and his preferred reading?

2/7 What is Harriet's favourite reading?

2/8 Who is Mr Elton's closest male friend in Highbury and who is his most devoted female admirer?

2/9 How many Emmas do we encounter in this novel?

2/10 What do 'little Bella' and Harriet Smith have in common?

2/11 Does Emma have a personal maid, and what do we know of her?

2/12 What, precisely, do we know of the Woodhouse family and pedigree?

2/13 Randalls is sometimes said to be three-quarters of a mile from Hartfield, and sometimes half a mile. How does one account for the difference?

2/14 'There are men who might not object to—' Harriet's illegitimacy, Mr Elton is about to say. How does he know she is illegitimate?

2/15 Where did Frank and Jane fall in love?

2/16 What 'trade' may we assume Mr Cole to be in?

2/17 Does Emma seriously suspect adultery, or adulterous intent, among the Weymouth set?

2/18 Why does Harriet hate Italian singing?

2/19 Why does Mr Knightley think Jane unattractive as a prospective wife (apart, of course, from her pennilessness and lack of acres)?

2/20 What is Jane Fairfax's 'daily errand'?

2/21 How is the visit to Hartfield by the two little boys Henry and John indirectly responsible for Mr Knightley becoming suspicious of Frank Churchill's behaviour towards both Emma and Jane Fairfax?

2/22 Who, as we are told, 'has always been rather a friend to the abolition [of the slave trade]'?

2/23 Who 'always travels with her own sheets'?

2/24 Why, if Selina Hawkins has made such a fine match with the owner of Maple Grove (with a barouche landau, to boot), does her sister Augusta have to make do with a relatively impecunious country clergyman? And why did she marry him so precipitately, without even looking over the living at Highbury where she would, probably, spend the rest of her life?

2/25 What prevents Harriet from running away, when confronted by thieving, dangerous gipsies?

☞ *Answers at the back of the book. Anything over 12 is good,*
  indicating either strong memory or recent acquaintance.
  Go on to Level Three ('Very Tricky—and Occasionally
  Deductive') which requires, in addition to intimate know-
  ledge of the text, an ability to make plausible deductions
  from it.

Level Three: Very Tricky—and Occasionally Deductive

3/1 Where does Mr Woodhouse's great wealth come from?

3/2 How old is Emma, and what does her age signify?

3/3 How old is Mr Woodhouse?

3/4 What do we know of Mr Weston and his background?

3/5 What feminine 'beauty' does Emma particularly admire?

3/6 Emma mentally divides society into four ranks: the poor, the yeomanry, the gentry, and the nobility. To which group does Robert Martin belong?

3/7 Robert Martin, we learn, has an 'unmodulated' voice and has no 'air', such as Mr Knightley has. What do these terms mean?

3/8 What do we know of Mr Elton's background?

3/9 'Men of sense', says Mr Knightley, 'do not want silly wives'. How, then, does he account for his very sensible brother John marrying very silly Isabella?

3/10 In conversation when, as Mr Knightley reports, 'there are only men present', Mr Elton has indicated his intentions of setting his hat at the daughters (twenty-thousand pounders, each of them) of a family with whom his sisters are intimate. Why then is he targeting Emma, and has he confided his intentions, about Miss Woodhouse, to Mr Knightley?

3/11 Who lives at Clayton Park?

3/12 How good a vicar is Mr Elton?

3/13 Why does Emma dislike Jane Fairfax—a young lady of high education and good breeding, whom she has known since childhood?

3/14 Desperate to change the subject in the epic Perry versus Wingfield physician controversy, Emma asks John Knightley about his friend Mr Graham bringing in a Scottish bailiff to manage his estate. But will it answer, she asks, 'will not the old prejudice be too strong?' What is the 'old prejudice'?

3/15 'She believed he had been drinking too much of Mr Weston's good wine'. It is one of the most famous lines in Austen. Why does not Emma know that Mr Elton has overindulged?

3/16 What, by her meaningful maiden name, do we assume Mrs Elton's family made their money in?

3/17 What was Frank Churchill doing at Weymouth, the previous autumn?

3/18 When he takes his farewell from Emma, and seems— standing at the window with his back to her—to be about to divulge something momentous, is Frank about to propose to Miss Woodhouse, or to confess his involvement with Miss Fairfax?

3/19 Who 'rather preferred an olive'?

3/20 What is the second occasion that gipsies are introduced into the action, the first being the assault on Harriet? What is the third?

3/21 There is some discussion of 'Swisserland' in the novel. Would it be possible to go there during the Napoleonic Wars?

3/22 Arrange Mr Woodhouse, Mr Elton, Mr Perry, and Mr George Knightley in ascending order of height.

3/23 Who has the management of (inept) Mr Woodhouse's huge wealth?

3/24 Robert Martin can dine with the John Knightleys in London. Why will he never (as the end of the novel prophesies) dine (along with his wife) with the George Knightleys in Highbury?

3/25 If Mrs Goddard knows Harriet's origins (she is the illegitimate daughter of a rich tradesman) why does Harriet herself not know?

☞ *Answers at the back of the book. The factual questions are very difficult, and some of the questions involve interpretation. If you score anything over 10, go forward to Level Four ('The Interpretative Zone'). If your deductive answers genuinely strike you as more convincing, or ingenious, than mine, give yourself a bonus point (or more).*

Level Four: The Interpretative Zone

4/1 Why is Emma so different in temperament from her sister Isabella and her father? Is there no genetic heritage in Austen's world—was DNA not a consideration before Crick and Watson discovered it?

4/2 What, educationally, has Emma had from her personal tutor, Miss Taylor, that Harriet has not acquired from Mrs Goddard?

4/3 Why does Emma particularly dislike Miss Bates—a woman whose 'simplicity and cheerfulness of nature . . . were a recommendation to everybody' (except, apparently, Miss Woodhouse)?

4/4 'I have always thought it a very foolish intimacy,' says Mr Knightley of Emma and Harriet's friendship, during his first quarrel with Emma (about her inducing Harriet to reject Robert Martin). He adds, 'though I have kept my thought to myself'. But we recall him saying to Emma's oldest friend (and intimate): 'I do not know what your opinion may be, Mrs Weston . . . of this great intimacy between Emma and Harriet Smith, but I think it a bad thing.' What should we make of this contradiction?

4/5 The John Knightleys come to Hartfield for Christmas, but only stay until the 28th of the month—because John 'has to be in town'. Are there any other deducible reasons for the shortness of the stay?

4/6 'I will have nothing to do with it', says Emma firmly, when Harriet asks for advice about how to respond to Robert Martin's letter of proposal. She then dictates her protegée's response. Does Emma know she is lying, or does she deceive herself in these circumstances?

4/7 When Emma asserts it would be a 'degradation' for Harriet to marry Robert Martin, Mr Knightley exclaims: 'A degradation to illegitimacy and ignorance, to be married to a respectable intelligent gentleman-farmer!' What are the socio-historical implications?

4/8 At one stage, Isabella has four children, later she seems to have five. How do we explain this?

4/9 What should we make of the Vicarage being 'an old and not very good house'?

4/10 Emma is 'compassionate' and visits Highbury's poor, to give them some genteel relief. Most of one chapter in this 400-page book is devoted to this worthy activity. Why, as the person of most consequence in her community, does she not do more?

4/11 The ostensible reason for Jane's coming to Highbury is to recover from a bad cold (contracted some months since). It is true her mother died of consumption, but what, may we surmise, were Jane's real reasons for not going to Ireland with the Campbell–Dixon party?

4/12 We are told that there is not a creature in the world to whom Emma speaks with such 'unreserve' as Mrs Weston (whom she sees 'every day'). Has she confided to her the marital project for Harriet Smith? Is Mrs Weston her accomplice?

4/13 What is the name of the family who, if they visit Enscombe, will oblige Frank Churchill to forgo his visit to Highbury?

4/14 'Oh, Mrs Churchill,' exclaims Isabella, 'every body knows Mrs Churchill'. Do they? And how?

4/15 Why are the Woodhouses 'first in consequence' at Highbury when they have no land, no grand house, no title? Mr Woodhouse is not (like Mr Knightley) a squire or a JP. What, then, is their 'consequence'?

4/16 Where do the Bates ladies (and, presumably, their niece Jane) stand in the Highbury hierarchy, and who owns their home?

4/17 What kind of farmer is Mr Knightley?

4/18 How many characters in Jane Austen do we know to wear spectacles, and what is the only work we ever see Frank Churchill carrying out?

4/19 It is clear from the Donwell picnic that Emma rarely visits the Abbey. Why not?

4/20 What other functions than Frank Churchill's ball take place at the Crown Inn?

4/21 Why does Mrs Weston think so highly of Jane Fairfax?

4/22 What is John Knightley's gruff commendation of Britain's excellent postal service?

4/23 Austen previewed, in her mind, the novel as a three-volume affair—each volume having to 'sell itself' to the library subscriber. What are the big events of the respective volumes?

4/24 When Frank instructs Emma to choose a wife for him with the words 'I am in no hurry. Adopt her, educate her', are we to assume that he has seen through her Harriet matchmaking ruse?

4/25 Mr Elton wanted to marry Emma. Does (the Revd) Mr Elton at least marry Emma and Mr Knightley?

☞ *Check answers at the end of the book. Give yourself a bonus for every interpretative answer which seems to you (1) correct (2) more plausible, witty, or ingenious than that which I offer.*

Total all your marks. If you scored 100 (or more), write your own book. Over 60, congratulations; 30 or less—you will have the pleasure of rereading Emma.

Persuasion

Introductory Note on the Novel

Persuasion was Jane Austen's last completed novel, written between summer 1815 and summer 1816. In 1816 the author fell into the lingering illness which eventually killed her, in July 1817. Austen herself may have suspected the plot lacked her normal sparkle, since she thought the original ending was 'tame and flat', and rewrote it (the revised ending has a number of hanging threads which, perversely, leave a piquant taste). In March 1817 she told her niece Fanny Knight that she had another novel ready for publication, but added: 'You will not like it, so you need not be impatient. You may *perhaps* like the Heroine, as she is almost too good for me.' Discriminating critics have, more often, found it her most mature—if least funny—work. The novel was published posthumously in a four-volume bundle along with *Northanger Abbey* (her least mature work), by John Murray, in December 1817 (dated 1818 on the title page), together with an informative 'Biographical Notice of the Author' written by Jane's brother (and sometime unofficial literary agent) Henry Austen. The novel's action can be precisely placed (thanks to the *Baronetage* entry on the first page) as being over nine months, summer 1814 to spring 1815.

Level One: Brass Tacks

1/1 How old is Anne Elliot?

1/2 What is the dominant element in Sir Walter's character?

1/3 Why is the period (1814) propitious for the letting out of fine country houses like Kellynch Hall? And who duly rents the establishment?

1/4 How are the Crofts related to the Wentworths?

1/5 What is Mrs Clay's connection with the Elliot family?

1/6 What rank was Lady Russell's departed husband?

1/7 What formal schooling has Anne received?

1/8 What profession was Frederick Wentworth's father?

1/9 Why cannot Anne accompany the Charles Musgroves on their first visit to the Crofts at Kellynch Hall?

1/10 How do Anne and Frederick greet each other, after eight years' separation?

1/11 How many Charleses are there in the novel, and how many Walters?

1/12 How often has Mary Musgrove been in her relatives', the Hayters', house at Winthrop?

1/13 Has Anne ever visited Lyme before?

1/14 What is Lady Russell's favourite recreation?

1/15 What is the 'domestic hurricane' in the Musgrove household?

1/16 Bath rings to the bawling of street vendors (such as muffin-men and milk-men) and the 'ceaseless clink of pattens'? What are these?

1/17 What does Sir Walter regret in his heir, William's, other-wise satisfactory appearance?

1/18 How long must Mr William Elliot decently mourn his deceased wife, before being able to remarry?

1/19 How big is the blister on Mrs Croft's heel?

1/20 What, in Admiral Croft's view, is James Benwick's principal failing?

1/21 What kind of acquaintance does Sir Walter tell the Dalrymples he has with Captain Wentworth?

1/22 How old is William Elliot?

1/23 How much has Captain Wentworth in prize money, to support him in civilian life?

1/24 When Captain Harville tells Anne 'if I could but make you comprehend what a man suffers when he takes a last look at his wife and children, and watches the boat he has sent them off in, as long as it is in sight, and then turns away and says, "God knows whether we ever meet again!",' what, exactly, is he picturing?

1/25 What is Anne's final good turn in the novel to those less fortunate than her lucky self?

☞ *Check answers at the back of the volume. If you scored over 15, proceed to Level Two ('Factual but Tricky'). If you scored over 10 but under 15, skim the novel again. Over 5 but under 10, reread the novel. Under 5, throw this book away and watch TV.*

Level Two: Factual but Tricky

2/1 Does Anne take after her mother, or her father?

2/2 When did Anne and Frederick first become attracted to each other?

2/3 Could Anne, had she been stronger willed, have married the young Commander Wentworth (as he then was)?

2/4 Who is Sir Walter's favourite and who his least favourite daughter, and why?

2/5 Why should Sir Walter (whose income, when managed by Lady Elliot's good sense, was quite adequate) be 'distressed for money'?

2/6 What naval action do we know Admiral Croft to have been in, and what naval action Captain Wentworth?

2/7 What are the principal residences at Uppercross?

2/8 What is the only period of her domestic existence when Anne can be said to have been happy?

2/9 What, precisely, were Dick Musgrove's delinquencies which resulted in his being so happily dead before his twentieth year?

2/10 Why is everyone so alarmed at little Charles Musgrove dislocating his collar bone?

2/11 Why is Frederick Wentworth 'lucky' (as Admiral Croft thinks) to get command of the sloop *Asp* when still in his twenties?

2/12 Who are the best scholars in the novel?

2/13 There is one reference to excrement in Jane Austen's six major novels. Where is it to be found?

2/14 Where is Captain Harville wounded?

2/15 Is it the loss of his beloved Fanny Harville which has turned Captain Benwick to poetry and melancholy?

2/16 Who has the better manners, Captain Harville or Captain Wentworth?

2/17 What causes the years' long rupture between the Dalrymples and the Elliots?

2/18 What is Mrs Smith's connection with Anne, and what is she doing at Bath?

2/19 How long is it since Mrs Smith saw Mr William Elliot, and why does she want Anne to intercede with him, on her behalf?

2/20 For how much would William Elliot, as he protests (according to Mrs Smith), sell his baronetcy, were the title saleable?

2/21 What makes it possible, at last, for Charles Hayter to make a legitimate bid for Henrietta Musgrove?

2/22 What finally reconciles Charles Musgrove to his future brother-in-law, the bookish Benwick?

2/23 What finally reconciles the snobbish Elizabeth Elliot to Frederick Wentworth?

2/24 What is the ostensible letter Captain Wentworth is penning, as he is actually tumbling out his declaration of undying love to Anne?

2/25 Does Lady Russell admit, finally, that her 'persuasion' was wrong?

☞ *Answers at the back of the book. Anything over 12 is good, indicating either strong memory or recent acquaintance. Go on to Level Three ('Very Tricky—and Occasionally Deductive') which requires, in addition to intimate knowledge of the text, an ability to make plausible deductions from it.*

Level Three: Very Tricky—and Occasionally Deductive

3/1 What, in terms of personal attraction, has the 27-year-old Anne Elliot lost?

3/2 Who is the heir presumptive of Kellynch Hall, and why did he not, as designed by Sir Walter, marry Elizabeth?

3/3 When Elizabeth tells her sister, by way of praise of her father's nobility, that he 'has kept himself single so long for our sakes', what does she mean?

3/4 We are told that Charles Musgrove does 'nothing with much zeal, but sport'. What else can he be said to do?

3/5 When Mary Musgrove, justifying her leaving her sick child, says, 'his papa can, and why should not I?', is it to be read as the rationalization of a bad mother, or the argument of a sensible woman?

3/6 When Frederick Wentworth returns, on indefinite shore leave, and tells his sister that any woman 'between fifteen and thirty may have me for the asking' what would she deduce about his state of mind?

3/7 *Persuasion* could perhaps be subtitled, like Sheridan's play, *The Rivals*. How much do the various lovers in the narrative know about their rivals?

3/8 Does Mary Musgrove know that Charles took her simply because Anne refused him and she (younger, and less beautiful) was next in line (and, for the union of the two estates, a Musgrove–Elliot match was desirable)?

3/9 What injury does Louisa sustain at Lyme Regis?

3/10 What is the Crofts' principal attraction to Anne, as tenants of Kellynch Hall?

3/11 What changes, of a minor kind, do the Crofts make to Kellynch Hall, to fit it for their habitation?

3/12 Why does Mary insist on remaining (instead of Anne) with the invalid Louisa, convalescent with the Harvilles, given her general uselessness and proclivity towards hysterics?

3/13 What support does Mrs Smith have, to keep herself genteel?

3/14 What, in Sir Walter's view, will 'surprise' Westgate Buildings, where Mrs Smith resides, in the old quarter of Bath?

3/15 What, in Anne's analysis, accounts for the union of the bookish Benwick and the very light-headed Louisa?

3/16 How is it that Mrs Smith is so 'penetrating' on the subject of Anne's personal situation at Bath—notably her suspicion that her friend is in love?

3/17 Anne, for (an impressed) William Elliot's benefit, translates the words of an Italian song they have been listening to. Where has she learned the language?

3/18 What is the one violation of the 'laws of honour' for which the reader can indict Anne Elliot?

3/19 What term of address does Anne use towards her father?

3/20 Will the several captains (three of them) remain in the naval service, after the narrative reaches its romantic conclusion— professions often lasting longer than love?

3/21 What is Mary's ostensible reason, and what may we assume her covert reason, for approving of Anne's marriage to Frederick?

3/22 What will happen, we apprehend, to Mr Shepherd?

3/23 What reason does Captain Wentworth give for not having proposed again to Anne when he returned, 'in the year eight, with a few thousand pounds' and what would have happened had he done so?

3/24 Will Anne and Frederick have children?

3/25 What, finally, happens to Elizabeth Elliot?

☞ *Answers at the back of the book. The factual questions are very difficult, and some of the questions involve interpretation. If you score anything over 10, go forward to Level Four ('The Interpretative Zone'). If your deductive answers genuinely strike you as more convincing, or ingenious, than mine, give yourself a bonus point (or more).*

Level Four: The Interpretative Zone

4/1 Is 'persuasion', as a moral instrument, good or bad?

4/2 *Persuasion* is unusual in not having the rather loose dating frame which contains, for example, the opening of *Mansfield Park* ('About thirty years ago . . .'). The opening page of *Persuasion* informs us (principally via the family entry in the *Baronetage*) that Sir Walter was born in 1760 and is now 54; that Anne, the 'persuaded' (in 1806) heroine was born in 1787 and is now 27. Why this chronological precision?

4/3 Why does Sir Walter object to sailors and their current popularity as heroes of the war and saviours of their country?

4/4 In Jane Austen's fiction, married women often have what we would see as psychiatric disorders—*vide* Lady Bertram's 'indolence' and Mrs Bennet's 'nerves', Mrs Norris's kleptomania. What, if anything, should we read into Mary Musgrove's chronic hypochondria?

4/5 There is a long rhapsody, by Frederick Wentworth, on his first command, the *Asp*. It is the first occasion in the novel on which he may be said to be eloquent. What about the *Asp* particularly recommends it?

4/6 Why does Frederick Wentworth, a gallant sailor who has been under fire, seen men killed alongside him, and taken French ships in battle, behave like a helpless girl when Louisa falls and bangs her head, jumping from the Cobb?

4/7 Lady Russell does not catch sight of Frederick Wentworth all the months he is visiting and staying at Kellynch Hall. She and Anne come across him (Lady Russell for the first time since 1806) in Pulteney Street. Does Lady Russell recognize him then?

4/8 Overheard conversation plays a major part in the plot of *Persuasion*. Anne, for example, happens by chance to be behind a hedge and hears Frederick lecture Louisa, at great length, on the moral quality of the hazel nut. What, relevant to Anne's personal attractions, is accidentally overheard about her at Molland's shop in Bath?

4/9 What are Mrs Smith's motives in renewing, so intensely, her friendship with Anne and how do her motives change as the friendship is renewed?

4/10 What can the reader put together of William Elliot's back story?

4/11 Why does Mrs Smith keep the letter of William Elliot's to Charles Smith, of July 1803, in which he is so coarsely rude about Sir Walter and Miss Elliot and so frank about his mercenary motives?

4/12 What does William Elliot protest, in his letter to Charles Smith, will be the purpose of his first visit to Kellynch Hall as the new baronet?

4/13 What puts it impulsively into Wentworth's mind to write a love letter so late in the day? Why is the letter to Anne so passionate and tumultuous?

4/14 One of the questions raised, tantalizingly, at the conclusion of the novel, in the conversation between Harville and Anne (as Wentworth, in another part of the room, is writing his love letter), is whether man or woman loves most faithfully. Who has the better of the argument?

4/15 What should one make of Anne's retort to Harville's remarks about the universality, in literature, of the refrain that woman is constitutionally inconstant: 'Men have had every advantage of us in telling their own story'?

4/16 Is it a failure of invention, or perhaps a mark of exhaustion, that Jane Austen cannot devise some means by which Kellynch Hall should revert to its 'true' custodian, Anne Elliot (as, we assume, Mansfield Park will one day revert to the Edmund Bertrams)?

4/17 The first report Anne hears Wentworth has made about her, after eight years' separation, is that she is so altered he should not have known her again. Yet, in their final reconciliation, he protests, 'to my eye you could never alter'. Is he mis-speaking?

4/18 We learn, in the last pages, that William Elliot has been playing a very cunning double game. What is that game, and why is he playing it?

4/19 How did William Elliot 'ruin' Charles Smith?

4/20 What are we to make of the final sentences about the elopement of William Elliot and Mrs Clay: 'She has abilities, however, as well as affections; and it is now a doubtful point whether his cunning, or hers, may finally carry the day; whether, after preventing her from being the wife of Sir Walter, he may not be wheedled and caressed at last into making her the wife of Sir William'?

4/21 Mary's gratification at Anne's being finally married is, we are told, slightly marred by her 'seeing Anne restored to the rights of seniority, and the mistress of a very pretty landaulette'. What may we read into these details?

4/22 Is 'war', as the novel presents it, a good thing?

4/23 What, in the foreseeable future, will happen to Kellynch Hall?

4/24 Are we to assume that Anne will be—in future years— another Mrs Admiral Croft?

4/25 Jane Austen's aphorisms are famous and often richly ironic. What can one read into the last sentence of *Persuasion*?

☞ *Check answers at the end of the book. Give yourself a bonus for every interpretative answer which seems to you (1) correct (2) more plausible, witty, or ingenious than that which I offer.*

Total all your marks. If you scored 100 (or more), write your own book. Over 60, congratulations; 30 or less—you will have the pleasure of rereading **Persuasion**.

THE ANSWERS

Sense and Sensibility

Level One

1/1 *Under what circumstances did the Henry Dashwood family move in with Henry's uncle, old Mr Dashwood?* He was unmarried, and when his sister, who was also his housekeeper, died, he invited the Henry Dashwoods (wife, husband, three daughters) to move in with him as his future heirs, and the companions of his old age. They sold all the furniture in their house, Stanhill, keeping only the linen, china, and plate (wedding presents, presumably). We may suspect that the Henry Dashwoods are not prosperous. Henry's second marriage is to a woman much younger than himself (she is still a nubile late-thirty-something, at the beginning of the narrative). He, we assume, with a grown-up son from a first marriage, is probably at least a decade older. After ten years of this shared family life, old Mr Dashwood dies, leaving a life interest in the Norland estate to Mr Henry Dashwood.

1/2 *How much money do the Dashwood women have between them, and how much do each of the three daughters individually possess?* On his premature death, Henry Dashwood leaves his wife £7,000. His daughters are left £1,000 apiece by their great-uncle. This will yield, as we are precisely informed, an annual income (from the Consols) of £500.

1/3 *How much does the Norland estate yield annually to its new owner, Mr John Dashwood?* A cool £4,000 a year. As the tenant-for-life he evidently feels free to cut down its 'valuable woods', starting with the 'old walnut trees' to make way for a conservatory and flower garden. Luckily, Marianne is not present when John Dashwood talks of this modernizing vandalism.

1/4 *Mr John Dashwood's first intention was to honour his father's deathbed wish by giving his half-sisters £3,000. How much, after* *being persuaded by his mercenary wife on the matter, does he finally resolve to give them? And how much does he actually come across with?* The couple eventually decide that a 'a present of fifty pounds, now and then' will be appropriate. It never materializes.

1/5 *What is the largest and most cumbersome object the Dashwood ladies have to transport to Barton Cottage?* Marianne's pianoforte.

1/6 *In which month of the year do the Dashwood ladies arrive at Barton Park?* September. The fact that it is late in the year means that (1) Mrs Dashwood cannot immediately carry out her 'improvements' (the implication is that, as in Sterne's Shandy Hall, they never will happen); (2) with the onset of winter, the fallow season, and long nights there will be the field sports and evening parties which 'social' Sir John loves. It may well be that he invited the ladies to his estate with that in mind.

1/7 *What is Sir John's favourite term for handsome young girls (for whom he clearly has an eye)?* 'Monstrous pretty!'

1/8 *Mrs Jennings is a widow with 'an ample jointure'. What is that?* A life interest in property, settled on her by her deceased husband. She cannot dispose of it as she might wish, through a will. It will go to her children.

   Mrs Jennings is one of the two women in the novel (the other is Mrs Ferrars) who are in charge of considerable wealth, and the social power which goes with it. She seems to get on very well with both her daughters, different characters though they are. They, on their side, seem to get on very well with their mother (there is no mercenary interest, of course; the terms of their father's will make it clear the family wealth will eventually come to them). Such happy families are not found everywhere in Austen's fiction.

1/9 *What is Willoughby, a Somersetshire man, doing in Devon?* He comes down every year for the shooting (he is evidently friendly with Sir John) and to pay his addresses to his patroness and elderly cousin Mrs Smith of Allenham.

1/10 *What word sums up Lady Middleton?* Insipid.

1/11 *Where do the Miss Careys live?* Newton village.

1/12 *What time of day (according to Sir John Middleton) does Willoughby usually rise in the morning?* Noon. Sir John, who has doubtless been kept waiting to get out into the fields with his fellow sportsman, is probably exaggerating. When it comes to paying court to Marianne, Willoughby is quite capable of making a mid-morning call at Barton Cottage.

1/13 *Who, apart from Marianne, is Willoughby's 'inseparable companion' at Barton Cottage?* His pointer, a black bitch.

1/14 *Where does Edward Ferrars stay when he comes to Devon and where does his horse stay?* He in the cottage, the horse in the village. There is no stable at Barton Cottage, so Willoughby's proposed gift of Queen Mab to Marianne would have been a major expense.

1/15 *Mrs Ferrars has been trying to push Edward into taking up a profession. What has she suggested, what are his objections, and what does he eventually do, at the end of the novel?* Her first choice for him was the army, as being very smart; Edward felt 'it was a great deal too smart for me'. Her second choice was the law, as young barristers could likewise present a dashing appearence as men-about-town; Edward has no inclination for the law, nor is he interested in a political career. The navy 'had fashion on its side'; but at 18 Edward was already too old to sign on as a midshipman. He himself wanted to enter the Church, but 'that was not smart enough for my family'. He went to Oxford as a time-killing last resort, and now that he has left, has no occupation at all (other than potential bigamist). Eventually he does drift into ordination, thanks mainly to Colonel Brandon promising him the living of Delaford.

1/16 *What is the epithet most accurately applied to Charlotte Palmer?* Silly.

1/17 *Who (before Elinor is spitefully told) is the only other person who knows about the secret engagement of Lucy and Edward?* Nancy Steele.

1/18 *How much does the public postal service, for a letter, cost in the world of* Sense and Sensibility? Two pence within the area of London, considerably more for the countryside beyond London.

1/19 *What is Mrs Jennings's 'favourite meal'?* Breakfast (taken, at this period, around noon).

1/20 *What is given Marianne to relieve her 'hysteria', in the extremity of her disappointed love?* Lavender drops—smelling salts, designed to stimulate and revive (they were not taken internally).

1/21 *Whom does Mrs Ferrars intend her son, Edward, to marry, and how much is the young lady worth?* Miss Morton, the daughter of Lord Morton. She is worth £30,000—the second most valuable such property in *Sense and Sensibility*, after Willoughby's Miss Grey.

1/22 *Who is the taller child, William Middleton or Harry Dashwood?* William, although only Elinor is brave enough to say so among all the toadies in the ladies' withdrawing room.

1/23 *How, when she visits him at Cleveland, does Elinor find Mr Thomas Palmer changed?* He is polite.

1/24 *What are Willoughby's last words to Elinor?* 'God bless you!'

1/25 *What is the only fly in the ointment for Edward and Elinor in the vicarage at Delaford?* There is not enough good pasturage for their cows.

Level Two

2/1 *The first sentences of Miss Austen's novels are famously memorable ('It is a truth universally acknowledged', etc.). Can you remember that with which* Sense and Sensibility *opens?* 'The family of Dashwood had been long settled in Sussex.' It seems the most neutral of openings, until—as the story unfolds—we appreciate that the family of Dashwood with whom we are most closely acquainted are being cruelly unsettled and will never live in Sussex again. Paradise Lost, only Regained, we eventually discover, in Devon and Dorset.

2/2 *What may we assume old Mr Dashwood's (he who dies, at an advanced age, on the first page) first name to be?* Henry. It is the name both of his first heir, and John Dashwood's son (little 'Harry'), the putative heir of Norland. This is a novel about patrilinearity, hence there is no surprise in little Henry being so named. What is mildly odd is that John Dashwood is christened thus—he is far more likely to have been Henry as well. Maybe John was the name of a rich maternal grandfather or uncle.

2/3 *Who educated Elinor and Marianne?* When we meet them, they are self-educating, hunting down books wherever they can. But presumably (from hints as to her teaching Margaret) Mrs Dashwood has been their tutor. She, however, married young (Elinor is 19, and Mrs Dashwood around 40). She is obviously too well bred to have been a governess herself, but was probably the beneficiary of an excellent home education. Someone, clearly, has taught Elinor to draw and Marianne to play the pianoforte—a relatively new instrument at this date. Probably instructors were brought in for them at Norland, in the days when the sun shone on them in Sussex. Obviously the family wealth which has descended to Sir John Middleton has not reached his cousin, Mrs Dashwood.

2/4 *What qualities does Edward Ferrars possess?* It is easier to describe those he does not possess. He has no profession. He is 'not handsome', and Marianne thinks 'his figure is not striking'. He does not play any musical instrument, or sing (as Willoughby does, so seductively); he has never learned to draw. Is his pledging himself (explicitly to the one, implicitly to the other) to two young ladies the consequence of not being able to make up his mind, or having no mind to make up?

2/5 *What was Colonel Brandon an officer in?* A regiment in the East Indies, we later learn. It was a posting where the climate was hot and the mosquitoes troublesome. He was fourteen years abroad, during which time (to judge by his rheumatism and flannel waistcoats—undervests, that is) he has evidently lost his resistance to the English climate. It is particularly foul in *Sense and Sensibility*. There is more rain than in any other Austen novel.

2/6 *What do we know of Mrs Smith?* Only that she is 'an elderly lady of very good character'. She neither goes into, nor receives, society because, as Willoughby says, she is 'too infirm to mix with the world'. Judging by her subsequent verdict on Willoughby, she may be evangelically inclined and morally strict. She disapproves of bastardy. Willoughby uses her infirmity as the excuse for not introducing Marianne to her. It is slightly odd, since he takes Marianne to look over most of Allenham. Even if, during their tour of the house, he avoided Mrs Smith's suite of rooms, surely the servants would have told the old lady that the young gentleman had brought in a young lady and they had walked about everywhere? Did he have to bribe the housekeeper to keep quiet?

2/7 *What was Willoughby doing, walking up the High Church Down?* Shooting gamebirds, ominously enough, with two pointers. He's on the lookout for more than one kind of prey, we may assume.

2/8 *Is Willoughby's scooping the fallen Marianne up into his arms at* *her request?* No, he overcomes her 'modest' resistance. He may also, cad that he is, have examined her ankle and the leg it is attached to.

2/9 *Who is Marianne walking with, when she has her momentous fall?* Her sister Margaret. It is Margaret who leaves the garden gate ajar (out of haste and fright, presumably) symbolically opening the house to the villain who will cause them so much grief.

2/10 *In what way, before she knows the older woman, does Elinor think Lady Middleton is to be preferred over her mother?* She is more silent.

2/11 *What is the play of Shakespeare's that the Dashwoods were reading during evenings at Barton Cottage with Willoughby, and never completed?* It is *Hamlet*. Ophelia's madness, on being unaccountably deserted by her princely lover, will strike a sadly appropriate chord.

2/12 *Who says 'these bottoms must be dirty in winter' and what does the statement mean?* The unromantic Edward Ferrars, adverting to the muddiness of the bottoms of West Country valleys—where, as it happens, the Dashwoods have their cottage.

2/13 *What gift does the sycophantic Lucy make for little Annamaria Middleton?* A filigree basket, put together with tiny strips of paper. She may be 'illiterate' but clearly she is deft with her fingers.

2/14 *Why is Marianne so keen for cold weather to arrive in London?* It will end fox and stag hunting in the country and Willoughby (whom she first met shooting, and who keeps hunters) will come up to town. What she does not know, of course, is that he is already in London, 'stalking' her in her Berkeley Street apartments.

2/15 *Why does Mrs Jennings not attend the ball at which*

Willoughby so cruelly humiliates Marianne? The 'indisposition' (that is, pregnancy) of her younger daughter, who is about to deliver a son and heir for Mr Palmer.

2/16 *Who says 'And what good does talking ever do'?* Mrs Jennings, ironically enough, the great talker in the novel.

2/17 *Do we ever know Colonel Brandon's Christian name?* No. For a bonus point, think of the most suitable.

2/18 *Where do the Miss Steeles stay when in London?* At Bartlett's Buildings, in Holborn—palpably less genteel than the West End, where the Dashwoods and Middletons stay.

2/19 *Who says of whom: 'At her time of life, any thing of an illness destroys the bloom for ever! Her's has been such a very short one!'* John Dashwood, of Marianne. She is now just 17.

2/20 *What is Mrs John Dashwood's reaction on learning that her brother Edward is secretly engaged to Lucy Steele?* 'Violent hysterics'.

2/21 *Overhearing part of Elinor's conversation with Colonel Brandon about Edward's marriage, Mrs Jennings misunderstands who is to marry whom, and says later 'Mr Ferrars is to be the man'; what does she mean?* She thinks he is to be the officiating clergyman. Elinor, of course, knows he will be the bridegroom.

2/22 *When Elinor makes her delayed visit, after a week, to the John Dashwood household in Harley Street, she is 'denied'. What does this mean?* That the couple are 'not at home'. They are, of course. It is one of the 'lies of politeness' that Elinor's code sanctions.

2/23 *When Marianne thinks the end has come what is her dying wish?* To see her mother.

2/24 *What is Edward's 'simple' errand on his second visit to Barton Cottage?* 'Only to ask Elinor to marry him'.

2/25 *Which of the sisters is a mother at the end of the novel?* Neither. Marianne, however, is the patroness of a village. She also, of course, has a household to manage.

Level Three

3/1 *Where does Elinor's good sense come from? No one else in her immediate family seems to possess it.* From books, we assume. She has seen very little of the world (the girls may not even have gone to London before Mrs Jennings takes them). The point is made over and over in *Sense and Sensibility* that the Dashwood girls read. This is essentially a book about the benign influence of books. But, of course, it depends on the books.

3/2 *Why are Mrs Henry Dashwood and her daughters not on closer terms with the John Dashwood family?* We may surmise that John Dashwood married to disoblige his family. They do not like his wife. His mother-in-law, the rich and tyrannical Mrs Ferrars, has never met any of the Dashwood family. The Ferrars money, we deduce, came from trade. Or worse. None the less, towards the end of old Mr Dashwood's life, the John Dashwoods are permitted 'occasional visits' to show off Harry. This imp 'gained on the affections of his uncle, by such attractions as are by no means unusual in children of two or three years old; an imperfect articulation, an earnest desire of having his own way, many cunning tricks, and a great deal of noise'.

Another explanation for the alienation between these two branches of the family (and their not coming together at the wedding of the Dashwoods) may be chronological. The reader is never informed what John Dashwood's age is—merely that he married very young, and that little Harry is about 4–5 in the course of the story. Even if he had his own maternal inheritance, it is doubtful whether he would have married before the age of 21. If one then allows some five to six years for little Harry's conception, gestation, and infancy, this would make John Dashwood now somewhere between 27 and 30. Elinor, meanwhile, is around

19, suggesting a gap between the wives and families of some eight to ten years. When John Dashwood married Fanny, therefore, Mrs Henry Dashwood was busy with three small girls, and may well not have wanted to travel to London for the wedding. Weddings were anyway small private affairs at this period, so the absence would not have been in any way remarkable.

3/3 *Fanny Dashwood 'had never been a favourite with any of her husband's family'. Why not?* She is, we deduce, 'low'. In her second reported speech in the novel she says, for example, of her dying father-in-law, 'ten to one but he was light-headed'. The turf metaphor is very telling (possibly Fanny picked it up from Robert Ferrars). No Dashwood *lady* would ever use it. The Ferrars money is, presumably, tainted by trade.

3/4 *What does Mr Henry Dashwood say to his son, John, as he (Henry) is dying, about supporting his surviving women-folk?* There are two versions. John may have given 'a solemn promise', in response to this most earnest of paternal entreaties. Or it may be, as he later asserts, that his father 'only requested me, in general terms to assist them'.

This relates to a larger and perplexing feature of *Sense and Sensibility*—what one might call the 'Chinese whispers effect'. We never directly witness momentous events in the novel: the seduction of Eliza Williams, or the duel between Brandon and Willoughby, for example. These things, like earthquakes in a neighbouring country, can only be known seismographically. It is, depending on the reader's constitution, one of the pleasures—or frustrations—of reading Austen. It is a tribute to her ethical conviction as an artist that she never writes about things of which she has no direct or (more typically) personal knowledge.

3/5 *What is Edward Ferrars doing in his six months' stay at Norland, while the Henry Dashwood ladies are still in the house?* He is idling, escaping the mother with whom he normally lives in London (and who wants 'him to make a fine figure in the world'), avoiding the choice of any profession, and (ambiguously) paying court to

Elinor. He has, we gather, just graduated from Oxford the summer before. Mr Henry Dashwood died (as we can calculate) in January or February. Edward, we are told, came soon after John and Fanny moved into Norland, say about March. Mrs Dashwood and the girls stay on for six months until the atmosphere becomes too strained (around August, probably), then arrange to leave and arrive in Devon in September.

3/6 *Why does Sir John Middleton write to Mrs Henry Dashwood, out of the blue, inviting her to stay at Barton Cottage?* He has, we later learn, just lost a tenant and he requires someone in the cottage for 'company'. Two eligible young ladies (plus a handsome widow, and a demure girl on the brink of being presentable) will be a catch for the balls and parties he loves, of a winter.

3/7 *In what ways is Barton Cottage 'defective'?* The criticism is ironic—directed against the picturesque tendencies of Marianne. 'The building', we are told, 'was regular, the roof was tiled, the window shutters were not painted green, nor were the walls covered with honeysuckles.' In other words, a 'des res' *c.*1800. 'Cottage' did not, of course, mean for the Georgians the cramped accommodation of a small, ancient rural dwelling which it means for us today.

3/8 *How many bedrooms does Barton Cottage have, and what issues does this raise in the modern reader's mind?* The cottage has four bedrooms and two garrets. The three live-in servants (the two females sharing) will inhabit the garrets. One bedroom is kept spare for guests, and it is likely that Margaret shares a room with her mother, thus leaving a room apiece for the two older girls. Hence Elinor doesn't have to be kept awake by Marianne weeping all night after Willoughby's abandoning her. It is not until they go to London that the elder sisters share a room, in the home of Mrs Jennings. This gives Austen the opportunity to describe Elinor sitting up in the cold winter dawn to see a distraught Marianne scribbling and crying at the window.

3/9 *Willoughby, when we first meet him, is accompanied by two pointers. One of them, a 'black bitch', recurs in the narrative (Sir John has a particular fancy for the animal). What is this favourite pointer's name?* Folly, as in Goldsmith's verse, 'When lovely woman stoops to folly'.

3/10 *What does it mean that Marianne's figure is 'not so correct as her sister's' and that she has very brown skin?* The description 'not so correct' does not mean she was round-shouldered, flabby, or skinny, but that, for perfectionists in questions of feminine style, her form is not considered as good as Elinor's—even though Marianne is the taller (which renders her, as the text observes early on, the more striking of the sisters). It might be that Marianne is more buxom (or less stringently corseted) and thus more likely to attract the eye of a rake like Willoughby (or a connoisseur of the female form like Sir John ('monstrous pretty!') Middleton). Her 'very brown' skin should not suggest, as it might today, a love of sunbathing, or careless exposure of her face to the elements. She is a natural brunette, hence her skin tone is 'brown' in keeping with her dark hair and eyes. Elinor's face presumably is fairly pale pink, in keeping with the fair hair we later learn she possesses. There was a fashionable preference for 'pale' feminine beauty which rendered Marianne a shade (literally) less obviously attractive.

3/11 *Some six mothers are portrayed at some length in* Sense and Sensibility. *Which of them can be seen as the best?* They are: Mrs John Dashwood, Mrs Henry Dashwood, Lady Middleton, Mrs Palmer, Mrs Jennings, and Mrs Ferrars. Mrs Jennings is the kindest—as we eventually discover. Mrs Henry Dashwood is perhaps the best—although she has faults of impulsiveness and procrastination. She is also a less than vigilant guardian of Marianne's interests. She, like her daughter, is seduced by Willoughby's handsomeness—although, very late in the day, she claims (unconvincingly) to have seen something malign in his eyes.

3/12 *What is the name of the horse Willoughby intends to give*

Marianne, and what is the allusion in its name? Queen Mab; the reference is to Mercutio's speech in *Romeo and Juliet*—a meaningful text for young lovers. Queen Mab is, of course, a mare. Willoughby, doubtless, will mount a stallion.

3/13 *What, from Marianne's later utterances, may we deduce that Willoughby has told her about what life will be like at Allenham for the future Mrs Willoughby?* Marianne (who has hitherto revealed no interest in domestic economy) airily declares: 'two thousand a-year is a very moderate income . . . A family cannot well be maintained on a smaller. I am sure I am not extravagant in my demands. A proper establishment of servants, a carriage, perhaps two, and hunters, cannot be supported on less.' These, surely, are Willoughby's lordly accents.

3/14 *Mrs Henry Dashwood, as the relationship has (to her maternal eye) reached its crucial stage, is content that Willoughby and Marianne should be left alone—for what will surely be a proposal on his part. Normally, of course, they would be chaperoned. Is a proposal his intention?* We are never quite sure (is he?). It might well be that Mrs Dashwood's forcing his hand in this way frightens him. Willoughby makes his own decisions about such things. He later claims that a poison pen letter to Mrs Smith, disclosing his misdeeds with Eliza Williams, has necessarily obliged him to leave Devon. It is hard to see, however, that he could ever have married Marianne unless Mrs Smith (who has never met the Dashwoods) supported his union with her. And there is no likelihood that she will if he does not ask her. It may be that the tacit understanding between him and Marianne is that they must wait for the old lady's death. At the end of the novel we learn that Mrs Smith might well have consented if only Willoughby had been open about it. Openness, however, is not in his nature.

3/15 *No letter is expected by Marianne from Willoughby. Why not?* He is too canny, with breach-of-promise suits in view, to put anything on paper. He has, falsely one presumes, told her he will not write but come in person in a short time. Willoughby—

although clearly a literate man—never, apparently, puts pen to paper. The only letter of his which we are given sight of in *Sense and Sensibility* was composed not by him, but his intended, Miss Grey.

3/16 *Why does Edward Ferrars start in alarm when Marianne says, without any ulterior meaning, that he is 'reserved'?* She means he is reserved in character. Uncommunicative. He at first misunderstands her to mean that he is 'reserved for another'. Spoken for—which, of course, he is.

3/17 *What colour is Elinor's hair?* The plait of hair in Edward's ring, as we later learn, is a love-token given him by Lucy Steele. The colour of it is evidently sufficiently similar for Marianne to think it belongs to his sister Fanny Dashwood, but she is puzzled because it seems to be 'lighter and brighter' than Fanny's. This comment makes Elinor think it belongs to herself, and that Edward has somehow managed to acquire a lock of it unbeknownst to her. So we learn that not only Fanny, but both Elinor and Lucy are blondes—evidently Edward, like other gentlemen, prefers them. And Edward's hair? Probably mousy.

3/18 *What did the late Mr Jennings do by way of occupation?* He 'traded with success in a less elegant part of the town'. He was, that is, 'in trade' in a less fashionable quarter of London than Portman Square; presumably the East End, or the City. The Jennings clan are sanitizing themselves from the taint of trade as fast as the marriage laws of England will permit them.

3/19 *Where has Charlotte Palmer been educated?* 'At a great school in town'. Austen does not think much of such great schools, judging by the sarcasm about the 'landscape in coloured silks' which is all Charlotte's seven-year course of education has produced. Charlotte, though amiable, is both stupid and ill-educated.

3/20 *What kind of carriage does Charlotte Palmer have?* A barouche. The Rolls-Royce of Regency personal transport, capable of holding at least four inside and a passenger on the box. Mrs Jennings's conveyance (unidentified, but probably a coach with ample room for her amplitude) is, by contrast, comfortable, luxurious, and dull. It would hold three or four at most. John Willoughby has a 'fast' (in every sense) curricle—a vehicle for the driver and one passenger. By their carriages shall ye know them.

3/21 *What is Marianne's characteristic expletive, when surprised?* 'Good God!' or 'Gracious God!' It is the closest thing to profanity we encounter in the novel and strange to hear from a well-bred 16-year-old lady's lips.

3/22 *How much wealth does Miss Grey, Willoughby's intended, have to give to her prospective lord and master?* Fifty thousand pounds. A prize so rich cannot have fallen easily into Willoughby's possession—more so as the lady is neither old nor repulsive. He must have 'won' her against fierce opposition from other fortune-hunters.

3/23 *How, as a special mark of favour, does Mrs John Dashwood address Lucy Steele?* By her Christian name. Nancy Steele is the elder, so she must always be 'Miss Steele'. The younger would be 'Miss Lucy Steele' or 'Miss Lucy'; to be addressed just as 'Lucy' does imply almost familial relationship, no doubt an encouragement for Nancy to blurt out the tale of the engagement.

3/24 *How is Colonel Brandon's 'I am afraid it cannot take place very soon' understood by the eavesdropping Mrs Jennings, and how is it understood by Elinor, whom he is talking to in his calm voice?* Mrs Jennings understands him to mean he cannot marry Elinor immediately. Elinor understands him (correctly) to mean that Edward will not be able to marry Lucy Steele on the paltry £200 the Delaford living affords. (It later emerges, however, that it is sufficient for Edward to marry the more eligible Elinor.)

3/25 *What does Willoughby euphemistically call his seduction of*

Eliza, in describing it to Elinor? 'An affair, a connection—but I
need not explain myself farther.'

Level Four

4/1 *How should we read the title? Is it 'Sense versus Sensibility'? Or
is the conjunction the more neutral 'and' as in 'Duck and Green
Peas'? Which of the two heroines represents which moral quality and
which is finally endorsed?* This question is more difficult than it
seems since by the end of the novel the sisters effectively reverse
their moral characters. At the beginning, Marianne is portrayed
as all passionate sensibility and Elinor as entire good sense. But
at the conclusion, Marianne has—after shattering illness, disil-
lusionment, and simple growing up—become sensible. She
inflicts on herself a programme of 'rational instruction' which
impresses even her hyper-rational sister. Elinor, by contrast,
when finally told that Edward is hers melts into ceaseless and
uncontrollable weeping. Has Marianne 'matured'? Has Elinor
'retrogressed'? The novel prohibits easy response. Perhaps we are
to assume the sisters have been put in life's pillowcase and shaken
up, so each has some of the other's characteristics.

It is also necessary to register slippage in the implications of
these key terms in the novel. When we today say 'sensible', we
mean: rational, practical, serviceable, trustworthy, placid,
unemotional—or any combination of these. 'Sensible' shoes for
walking; 'sensible' clothes for travelling; 'She's so sensible, she's
bound to make a good nurse . . .' For Elinor and Marianne
Dashwood, 'sensible' would have meant something like our modern 'sensitive'—someone, that is, capable of 'feeling', whose
senses were alert and receptive, that is, sense-able. Elinor is certainly sensible in the early nineteenth-century use of the word—
although she is good at concealing her emotions. 'Sensibility', in
the historical period in which the novel was set, implies affectation,
sentimentality, self-indulgence in excessive emotions.

4/2 *How old are the four Dashwood women at the start of the*

narrative, and what should we read into their respective ages?
Mrs Dashwood is barely 40. Elinor is 19. Marianne is 16. Margaret
is 13. In one sense, this is a novel about the very short but all-
important phases and divisions of a woman's life at the period.
The pre-pubescent Margaret is invisible for most of the novel
(although she takes her cues from Marianne, and has 'come out'
at the end of the novel). She is also, at times, a useful functionary
in the plot. It is Margaret's childish tactlessness during a visit to
Barton Park which puts into circulation the fact that Edward is
now courting Elinor (eventually it will reach Lucy's ears, with
dramatic consequences). And it is Margaret's presence at home
which enables her elder sisters to go off to London together,
without any difficulty that poor Mama will be left all alone. The
post-marital (but still, presumably, fertile) Mrs Dashwood is a
faint presence—because, of course, her sexual allure has waned
and has not (as with the widowed Mrs Ferrars and Mrs Jennings)
been compensated with wealth. Marianne, shortly after menarche,
is 'wild'; the victim of her newly rampant hormones. Elinor has
learned to control these dangerous impulses—one could not, for
example, imagine a scenario in which the 16-year-old Marianne
was 'sense': this quality is the product of time. But women have
so little time. As Mr John Dashwood observes, the 'bloom' passes
so quickly.

4/3 *Old Mr Dashwood's will creates the principal complication of
the ensuing plot—leaving, as he does, only a life interest to his nephew
Henry (whose subsequent life is sadly short). What, as best as one can
reconstruct it, is the Dashwood family tree and line of inheritance it
creates?* John Dashwood is the male heir to Norland, and so is
little Harry after him. The Dashwood family can be described in
terms of four generations. Generation A: Mr Henry Dashwood
of Norland, bachelor; his spinster sister Miss (first name
unknown) Dashwood, lives with him; his younger brother
Mr (first name unknown) Dashwood, presumably of Stanhill,
marries and begets Generation B. This generation comprises
Mr Henry Dashwood (junior), nephew of old Mr Henry
Dashwood (Generation A), and therefore heir to Norland, living

at Stanhill pro tem. This Mr Henry Dashwood marries twice, begetting four children, who make up Generation C. In this generation, Mr Henry Dashwood (of Generation B) begets by his first wife, Mr John Dashwood. John Dashwood marries Miss Fanny Ferrars. By his second wife, Mr Henry Dashwood (of Generation B) has three daughters, whose story makes up the main part of the novel, Elinor, Marianne, and Margaret. These young ladies are, therefore, great-nieces of Old Mr Henry Dashwood. Generation D centres around little Harry Dashwood, son of John and Fanny. Little Harry is the great-great-nephew of Old Mr Henry, but the heir apparent. Old Mr Henry Dashwood wants to ensure that Norland will continue in the male line and that Mr Henry Dashwood, the younger, doesn't sell the estate. Hence the life interest. It would have proved satisfactorily valuable, had he lived long enough. Mr John Dashwood is also, presumably, only given in his turn a life interest after his father, as 'the whole was tied up for the benefit of the child', little Harry.

4/4 *Why does Sir John charge Mrs Henry Dashwood rent, albeit an 'uncommonly moderate' rent?* Two reasons. First, it is, as we apprehend, a modern cottage (and much larger than that word suggests to the twenty-first-century ear). More to Sir John's credit, by charging a minimal rent, he respects the 'independence' of the ladies (which also means that he does not have the moral responsibility of finding husbands for the girls).

4/5 *Is Mrs Jennings's inveterate addiction to match-making 'vulgarity' and nothing more?* Not entirely. Marriage is the principal means by which families like hers, enriched by trade, can rise. Mrs Jennings is a kind of social chess player, moving her pieces into ever more advantageous positions on the board.

4/6 *Deaths are significant moments in the world of* Sense and Sensibility—*the moment at which inheritances happen and riches are distributed. What do we deduce to be the life expectancy of wealth-holders in the class of genteel, idle, English people who inhabit the world of* Sense and Sensibility? Fifty-five seems to be the expected term. John Dashwood thinks Mrs Henry Dashwood (aged 40) will be doing well to last another fifteen years (to his wife's horror). Marianne believes, ungenerously, that Colonel Brandon, aged 35, 'may live twenty years longer'. Mr Henry Dashwood evidently died in his mid-50s. The only very old people in the novel are 'old Gibson', who is evicted from his farm by the unfeeling John Dashwood, and 'old Mrs Smith', Willoughby's patroness, whom no one has seen for years.

4/7 *What, apart from misadventure, may we deduce from Marianne's spraining her ankle?* She is impetuous (Elinor is much more prudent in her running). She slips and 'falls'—fallen women are distantly glimpsed in this novel (we shall hear later of her predecessor in Willoughby's affection, Eliza Williams, daughter of a fallen woman).

4/8 *Why is Colonel Brandon so concerned with the validity of 'second attachments'?* He is worried (with a tragic youthful love behind him) that a romantic like Marianne will believe that, like the swan, a true lover can only love once in a lifetime. She may be right; but is certainly impractical.

4/9 *When, against her will, Marianne turns down Willoughby's offer of Queen Mab, she communicates the bad news to him in a 'low voice'. How can Elinor (as she does) overhear this conversation and the telling fact that Willoughby addresses her sister by her Christian name?* Elinor is quite legitimately eavesdropping. She is, of course, careful not to leave them alone; even though, at this stage, she has no reason to distrust Willoughby. She is playing what is a necessary social role—that of chaperone. In Jane Austen, young eligible men and women are usually only alone together when a proposal of marriage is in prospect. See, for example, *Pride and Prejudice* where Mrs Bennet winks at Kitty to get her out of the way so that Mr Bingley can propose to Jane. Since Elinor is habitually sketching and drawing, her silent presence in the room is not oppressive. Later in the narrative, Elinor is severe with the luckless Nancy Steele, when she relays details of a conversation between Lucy and Edward: 'have you been repeating to me what you only learnt yourself by listening at the door? I am sorry I did not know it before; for I certainly would not have suffered you to give me particulars of a conversation you ought not to have known yourself.' There is, quite clearly, eavesdropping and eavesdropping.

4/10 *Austen does not directly relate what is said between Marianne and Willoughby in the meeting at which, everyone at Barton Cottage expects, he will propose. What, can we deduce, does he say about seeing Marianne in the future?* She blurts out, a little later, 'he told me that it might be many weeks before we meet again'. We may assume that he has give some false assurances. The villain.

4/11 *In what circumstances does the moral paragon Elinor think it proper to tell lies?* 'When politeness required it'. She is no George Washington. It lands her in some odd ethical dilemmas. She is obliged, for politeness, to agree that her odiously skinflint half-brother is 'generous', or the boorish Mr Thomas Palmer is 'civil'.

4/12 *How long does the 23-year-old Lucy Steele claim to have been 'engaged' to Edward Ferrars, and should we believe her?* Lucy claims that they have been betrothed for four years. Later, Mrs Jennings puts it as 'above this twelvemonth.' It's an intriguing contradiction. Who is fibbing? The cunning Lucy, or the weak-kneed Edward? Obviously, if he has kept the young woman waiting four years (during which her short 'bloom' may have run its course) he is a villain, if not quite as hardened a villain as John Willoughby. And, of course, if it is a year ago that he proposed to Lucy in Exeter he must have done so at precisely the point he was paying court to Elinor Dashwood at Norland Park. Elinor accepts the four-year estimate. It seems that Lucy is thinking of the four years overall that Edward stayed with them as her uncle's pupil—the engagement only being formally established between them as he left.

4/13 What demonstrates, in Lucy's interpretation of things, that they are indeed plighted? The fact that he has given her a portrait miniature of himself and that he sends her private letters. In the world of *Sense and Sensibility*, 'a correspondence between them by letter could subsist only under a positive engagement'. It may be deduced that, at an early stage of the relationship, Edward put something injudicious on paper which has, legally, tied him to Lucy (or possibly Nancy overheard something, which she stored away). Letters, of course, might be brought against him in a breach-of-promise suit. And corresponding 'privately' (without the permission of Lucy's guardian, Mr Pratt) represents a liberty which can only be legitimized by 'honest intentions'. The word 'correspond' had the subsidiary meaning of 'sexual intercourse' in the eighteenth century (there is a hangover in the term 'co-respondent' in twentieth-century divorce terminology). It is likely that Nancy Steele overheard Edward proposing to Lucy—indeed, Lucy may have set her up to eavesdrop, so supplying a witness to the fact. One can imagine Nancy then bursting into the room, full of false sisterly joviality, claiming Edward as a future brother—to his knee-knocking dismay, poor fellow.

4/14 What should we make of Mrs Jennings's comment 'Upon my word I never saw a young woman so desperately in love in my life! My girls were nothing to her, and yet they used to be foolish enough . . .'? Can the cold insipid Lady Middleton, we wonder, ever really have been in love with Sir John? Or can Charlotte ever have worried whether Mr Palmer loved her or not? She seems quite placidly to accept the idea that a marriage might have been arranged for her with Colonel Brandon.

4/15 Colonel Brandon says (rather paradoxically) that Marianne and Willoughby 'openly correspond' (that is, exchange private letters). How does he know? He saw a letter, in a servant's hand, leaving Berkeley Street, 'accidentally', as he later avers. Of course, Colonel Brandon could not read the address did he not, quite improperly, as we may think, take the letter from the servant and inspect it closely. It may be, however, that Marianne's handwriting is as flamboyant as the rest of her personality and 'John Willoughby, Esqr., Bond Street' was writ very large. Anthony Trollope's pillar box, still four decades in the future, made things much easier for young lovers of the female sex. Until its arrival, the post had to be taken from the house, with all the likelihood that the wrong eyes would see it.

4/16 *What, from the two hearts which he has won (Eliza's and Marianne's), do we deduce is Willoughby's principal taste in young women?* That they are very young. Both are just 16. Miss Grey, the heiress, is older. As he says, he can never really love her. In addition to his other villainies there is something paedophiliac about Mr Willoughby.

4/17 *Where does Colonel Brandon learn of Willoughby's infamous conduct towards Marianne?* In a stationer's shop in Pall Mall. It is significant that he is not at a jeweller's, a tobacconist's, or a tailor's shop. He is at a place where he can get writing materials. The detail stresses the huge premium put on literacy and its civilizing effect in this novel.

4/18 *Who, do we learn, was Colonel Brandon's 'first attachment' and what can we gather about her?* This is one of the melodramas set in the distant background to Jane Austen's rigorously undramatic narrative. The young lady who first won Colonel Brandon's heart was Eliza Williams, an orphan who was made ward of the Colonel's father, her uncle. She was rich. The family property, Delaford, was 'much encumbered' and needed investment. Unscrupulously, the Colonel's father coerced his niece (17 and under age) into marriage with his elder son. It was against her inclination. He was not a 'good father'. Colonel Brandon (as we know him) was the younger son, and had been bought a commission in a home-based regiment. Colonel Brandon and his cousin fell in love and planned to elope. The plan was discovered, and she was forced into marriage with the elder son. The father lived only a few months more and Colonel Brandon exchanged his commission and went to serve in the East Indies. The marriage which provoked all the upheaval was not happy. 'His pleasures were not what they ought to have been' (wine, women, and gambling we assume). He 'treated her unkindly'. Eliza, in retaliation, was unfaithful and became pregnant by another. He divorced her (at this date it could only be done by Act of Parliament, and the woman's manifest adultery was the most convenient grounds). The husband now had all the money. She, a fallen woman and penniless (having been cheated out of her 'legal allowance'), fell 'deeper in a life of sin' on being abandoned by her seducer. Prostitution, we gather. She ended up in a sponging house (debtors' prison) with her daughter, also called Eliza Williams. Terminally consumptive, she was nursed by Colonel Brandon whose 'greatest comfort' was that the woman he once loved was dying. 'Life could do nothing for her, beyond giving time for a better preparation for death.' Her divorced husband by now is dead and her money, ironically, has descended into the hands of—who else?—Colonel Brandon. On her death he uses it to put Delaford into apple-pie order.

4/19 *Willoughby later says it is impossible for him to marry Eliza Williams (junior). Why?* Because she has an illegitimate child that would stain his reputation, even though it is of his own begetting. And, of course, she has no fortune.

4/20 *Does anyone get injured or killed in the duel between Willoughby and Brandon?* No, 'we returned unwounded', Brandon tells Elinor. Did they then merely cross swords, formally and perfunctorily? Or was there some minor scratch—a pink on the guilty man's arm—which drew enough blood to satisfy honour? It seems to have been, given the provocation, a strangely anaemic affair, the more so given Colonel Brandon's professional expertise (as we imagine) with the tool of his trade.

4/21 *What is Elinor doing in Gray's in Sackville Street, and why is she doing it, when she unwittingly observes Robert Ferrars?* She is negotiating 'for the exchange of a few old-fashioned jewels' of her mother's. Pawning or selling them, we apprehend. Mrs Dashwood perhaps has insufficient funds from her £500 a year to give her daughters an adequate London allowance. The rather vague description could also, one might speculate, mean trading in some old-fashioned settings for more modern styles. It was quite normal to have heirloom stones reset in this way to suit the style of a new wife or inheritrix.

4/22 *What is Robert Ferrars doing at the Sackville Street jewellers?* Buying himself a rich toothpick-case. It would also, probably, contain his shaving gear. Toothpicks, much as the idea of them makes the modern skin crawl, were the favoured means of cleaning teeth among the sanitary middle classes. The Dashwood ladies would, discreetly, use them. Unless, that is, they intend to knock down their lovers with their breath. Abrasive tooth powders were available at the time, administered with a sponge.

4/23 *What does the incorrigibly mean Mrs John Dashwood give the Steele girls by way of personal gift?* Needle-books, 'made by some emigrant' (that is, some impoverished Frenchwoman in exile, perhaps an aristocrat, eking out a living with her needle). This is the sole reference in *Sense and Sensibility* to the French Revolution. Later Nancy refers to these receptacles as humble 'huswifes'.

4/24 *Who tells Mrs John Dashwood that Lucy Steele is engaged to be married to her brother, Edward?* Nancy. It is later suggested that it was accidental (she 'popt it all out'). But Nancy has kept the secret four years and, we may suspect, Lucy (who seems not to bear her sister any great grudge for the indiscretion) may have put Nancy up to it. Mrs John Dashwood and Mrs Ferrars must know some time, and both seem now to be well disposed towards her. She has, of course, miscalculated.

4/25 *Why, if he thinks Lucy Steele the 'merest awkward country girl, without style, or elegance', does Robert Ferrars go out of his way to call on her?* He wants to seduce her, thinking that, in her abandonment, she will be easy pickings for a man of the world like himself. She, ironically, seduces him. Into marriage.

Pride and Prejudice

Level One

1/1 *Describe, with their Austenish epithet (or characteristic mark) the five Bennet girls, in order of age.* 'Beautiful' Jane, 'quick' Lizzy, 'clever' Mary (who none the less lacks 'genius and taste'); Kitty (Catherine) is 'slight and delicate' and coughs (is she tubercular?); Lydia, the tallest, laughs and has dangerously high 'animal spirits'. Their ages range from 22 (Jane), 20 (Elizabeth), down to the coltish Lydia (15). All are 'out'. Out on the marriage market, that is.

1/2 *What does Mr Bingley wear on his first visit to the Bennets at Longbourn?* A blue coat. The colour indicates a certain (charming) lightness of character. Wickham possibly wears a blue coat to his wedding.

1/3 *How many sisters does Mr Bingley have?* Excited gossip, in advance of any social connection, claims there are five. Only the odious Caroline and the nonentity Louisa later appear.

The superfluity of women over men is one of the oddities of the *Pride and Prejudice* world. It is, of course, a time of war, when, on the home front, women outnumber men. 'The scarcity of men' is commented on later in the novel. The militia regiment at Meryton (providing a transient male population) enhances this impression of a paucity of eligible men. In the last sentences of the novel Jane Austen makes one of her very few historical references, when she mentions that 'the restoration of peace' will upset the career of Wickham (now a regular soldier) and the prospects of his wife, Lydia. This is, presumably, the Peace of Amiens, 1802. Wickham, we may surmise, may later atone for his sexual misdeeds by gallantry in the Peninsular War (like George Eliot's Arthur Donnithorne). He may even survive to fight and die at Waterloo, alongside Thackeray's George Osborne.

It is worth commenting on the distinction between regular servicemen and militia men. At this date there was no conscription, so young men did not have to join up unless they wanted to. Only the determined tough ones joined the regular army, the others joined the militia (raised for service at home, in the event of French invasion). Militia could swagger about in red coats safe in the knowledge they would not face action overseas.

1/4 *What is Mr Bennet's estate, Longbourn, worth, and who will eventually inherit it?* Two thousand pounds a year. In default of a male heir (Mrs Bennet gives up after the fifth daughter), it is entailed on a 'distant relation' (Mr Collins, as we later learn).

Longbourn has a farm attached, but Mr Bennet has no interest, apparently, in improving its crops and increasing its yields. His carriage horses do, however, double as agricultural beasts. He spends lavishly on his library, which obviously means much more to him than his fields. His sole rural pursuit seems to be shooting, so presumably he is sufficiently interested in his estate to keep a gamekeeper for his pheasant coverts.

1/5 *How old is Charlotte Lucas?* Twenty-seven, ominously. Mrs Bennet ascribes Charlotte's misfortune to her being 'plain'—a Lucas family characteristic. Now, perhaps, Charlotte is too old for marriage. She is one of the clever women in Jane Austen afflicted with stupid parents and at least one stupid sister (Maria).

1/6 *What first begins to attract Darcy to Elizabeth?* Her fine dark eyes and her brilliant complexion (usually a primary attraction in Austen's heroines).

1/7 *Who is the commanding officer of the militia regiment which has been posted to Meryton for the winter, and who is the regiment's second in command?* Colonel Forster and Captain Carter.

1/8 *Where do the Bennet girls get their reading matter?* Clarke's library, in Meryton. It is also a good place to meet militia officers.

Mary evidently raids her father's library. Elizabeth declares that she is not a great reader (although clearly literate).

1/9 *What relation is Mr Philips to Elizabeth, and what is his profession?* Maternal uncle by marriage. He succeeded her maternal grandfather in his practice as a country attorney in Meryton.

1/10 *Who introduces Wickham to the Bennet young ladies, and what do we know of him?* Mr Denny (that is, a lieutenant, with 'Mr' as his military title, like Wickham). Having served his purpose in the plot he disappears. Later, although he may have been a party to the elopement of Wickham and Lydia, he claims ignorance.

1/11 *How much did the chimney-piece in Lady Catherine's drawing-room cost?* Eight hundred pounds. This seems a vast cost, unless it were plundered from some castle in Italy. It might conceivably be a printer's error for £300 (in figures in the manuscript). Or perhaps it is just another Mr Collins absurdity.

1/12 *How much does Wickham estimate that Pemberley is worth?* A 'clear' £10,000 a year. Bingley, the other very rich person in the novel, has a lump sum of £100,000 which would yield, from conventional investment, some £4,000–5,000 a year. Bingley, however, has no property to keep up.

1/13 *How much money does Mr Collins lose at whist?* Five shillings. Quite a sum, for a country clergyman.

1/14 *What is Sir William's favourite epithet?* 'Superior'. He feels, with some justice, a haunting sense of his own indelible inferiority, despite the presentation to his monarch at St James's.

1/15 *What are Mary's shortcomings as a singer and pianist?* As a singer, her voice is weak and her manner affected. As a pianist, she has 'a pedantic air and conceited manner'. Listening to her performing in public plunges Elizabeth into 'agonies' of familial shame.

1/16 *What does Mrs Gardiner inform her sister-in-law is the latest style in fashionable London?* Long sleeves. Presumably the needles start moving at once in Longbourn.

1/17 *To whom does the faithless Wickham transfer his affections, and why?* Miss King, who has, through her grandfather's recent death, come by £10,000. We know little else of Miss King beyond this all-important fact and that she is (as spite portrays her) 'a nasty little freckled thing'.

1/18 *How old is Elizabeth?* 'I am not one and twenty'.

1/19 *How far is it from Longbourn to Hunsford?* 'Nearly fifty miles'—of 'good road'. Austen is precise about such details, and evidently used road maps.

1/20 *What is George Wickham's relationship to Fitzwilliam Darcy?* None. George is old Mr Darcy's godson (the gentleman's name, quite likely, was George Darcy, we may deduce). Fitzwilliam is old Mr Darcy's son.

1/21 *How old is Darcy?* He is 28, which makes him thirteen years the senior of his 15-year-old sister (effectively, his ward) and some seven years older than Elizabeth.

1/22 *Why cannot Lydia buy lunch for Elizabeth and Jane, when she meets them at an inn on their return from London?* The little hussy has spent the money on a bonnet ('ugly' as Elizabeth and Jane think).

1/23 *Where does the ——shire militia go in the second week in May, after wintering at Meryton?* To the encampment at Brighton—for exercise or active service, we assume. Lydia goes with them, as a kind of camp-follower in training, with the light-headed wife of Colonel Forster.

The encampment at Brighton is one of the historical dating points for the composition of the novel, and its action. The camps at Brighton were only held in 1793, 1794, 1795, 1796, 1798, and 1803. Jane's brother Henry Austen was there in 1793 with the Oxfordshire militia, and the North Hants militia were also there that year—facts which evidently supplied her with information on camp life. Jane Austen fills in aspects of the social life of the militia via the younger Bennet sisters' connection with the commanding officer's family. We learn, for example, that Mrs Forster is 'a very young woman' (younger, presumably, than her husband who has risen in the service), light-headed, 'exuberant', and given to scheming. She takes a shine to Lydia (but not to Kitty, whom she does not invite to go with her at Brighton). Colonel Forster, by contrast, is a 'sensible man'.

1/24 *Why does Jane have to cede her place to Lydia, six years her junior?* 'Because I am a married woman', Lydia says.

1/25 *Why does Mr Bennet advise Mr Collins to 'stand by the nephew'?* Because 'he has more to give' (than Lady Catherine, in clerical preferments, that is).

Level Two

2/1 *Lizzy is described as 'trimming a hat'. What does this indicate?* A certain frugality, deftness with her fingers (she talks about their facility over the piano keys, elsewhere), and a kind of pride in her outdoor appearance (she is described as 'running' across fields, and 'jumping' stiles). Much later in the novel, Lydia is described as 'adding' ribbons to her hat, which suggests a vanity lacking in Lizzy.

2/2 *How has Sir William Lucas enriched and ennobled himself?* He was 'formerly in trade in Meryton'. He was ennobled by having presented a 'Loyal Address' to the monarch (George III) during his mayoralty. Sir William's being knighted at St James's, as he frequently recalls, was the high point of his public life. We assume, from his inability to give Charlotte a decent portion (which induces her to accept the odious Collins) that he is not all that rich—or not so rich that he can be generous to all his large family.

2/3 *What card-game do Jane and Bingley find they prefer?* Pontoon, blackjack, or—as they call it—Vingt-un. Bingley does not like the card game Commerce, which may be a clue as to where his money comes from.

2/4 *Why does Elizabeth not play loo with the Bingley sisters?* Because she suspects them 'to be playing high'. For money, that is—gambling for high stakes.

2/5 *Why is Miss Bingley so very keen to mend Darcy's pen, as he is writing a letter to his sister?* Two possible reasons. She is curious about what he is writing and hopes to catch a glimpse of his paper. And she wants to get his attention, hoping perhaps accidentally to tangle her fingers in his when she hands back the 'mended' quill. He is, of course, quite capable of sharpening the quill with his penknife himself.

2/6 *What news do Lydia and Kitty bring Jane and Lizzy from Meryton, when the older sisters return from visiting Netherfield?* That 'a private had been flogged' and that Colonel Forster is going to be married.

2/7 *How long has Mr Collins been ordained, when he writes to Mr Bennet on 15 October?* Since Easter. He is a mere 'five and twenty'—barely out of university. The living at Hunsford evidently came to him fortuitously. Why Lady Catherine should have chosen him (other than his pleasing sycophancy) is mysterious. Possibly she knows some Fellows of Mr Collins's college, and told them to find her a suitably meek young ordinand for her living, who could therefore be relied upon to be eternally grateful to her.

2/8 *How old is Georgiana Darcy?* 'A handsome girl, about fifteen or sixteen'.

2/9 *What is the connection of Lady Catherine de Bourgh and Lady Anne Darcy (deceased)?* They were sisters. Oddly, Mr Collins—who is fanatically attentive to everything connected with his patroness—does not know that Mr Darcy is the nephew of Lady Catherine.

2/10 *How much money do we learn (from Mr Collins, who has taken care to find out) Elizabeth will bring to her marriage? And how much will Charlotte bring?* Elizabeth will bring £1,000 in the '4 per cents.' (that is, government guaranteed bonds), after her mother's death. Sir William's affairs are not going well. Charlotte will bring 'very little'.

2/11 *Why, as the narrator uncompromisingly informs us, does Charlotte accept Mr Collins, and what is Elizabeth's one-word expletive on hearing that (three days after proposing to her, Miss Bennet) he has offered himself to Miss Lucas?* She 'accepted him solely from the pure and disinterested desire of an establishment'. Elizabeth's response, on being informed of her best friend's impending marriage is 'impossible!' On more mature reflection her verdict is 'unaccountable!' It is of course entirely accountable. How, one wonders, has Elizabeth so misunderstood her friend?

2/12 *Why does Mr Gardiner, Mrs Bennet's brother, come to Longbourn, and what do we learn of him?* He visits Longbourn to celebrate Christmas with the Bennets. Mr Gardiner is 'a sensible, gentlemanlike man, greatly superior to his sister as well by nature as education'. He lives by trade, and has 'warehouses' (a mercantile profession, we deduce). He is married and has a 'troop of little boys and girls' (four, to be precise) whom he has left in London (odd as this may seem to modern parents).

2/13 *What is Mrs Gardiner's connection with Pemberley?* About 'ten or a dozen years ago' she had spent considerable time in Derbyshire in the little town of Lambton near Pemberley. Her sage advice to Elizabeth—that she should not consider Wickham as a suitor—is on the mercantile grounds that neither party has sufficient wealth to marry ('I have nothing to say against *him*').

2/14 What is Mr Collins's favourite recreation? Hunsford Parsonage has a 'large and well laid out' garden 'to the cultivation of which he attended himself.' One of his 'most respectable pleasures', the narrator darkly adds.

2/15 Is Rosings a venerable old building? No, it is a handsome modern building. It is never entirely clear whether Jane Austen prefers the amenity of modernity, or the dignity of antiquity, in great houses. In addition to the vulgarly expensive chimney-piece in the drawing-room, allusion is made to the expensive 'glazing'.

2/16 When Lady Catherine asks, 'Are any of your younger sisters out, Miss Bennet?', what does the old battleaxe mean? She enquires whether they are on the marriage market. She is astonished to learn that all five (including 15-year-old Lydia) are 'out' and yet Jane, the eldest, is unmarried. The Lucas girls, Maria and her younger unnamed sisters, are meanwhile having to wait for their 'coming out' until Charlotte gets married. Lady Catherine de Bourgh is hard-headed as well as hard-hearted.

2/17 Why cannot Colonel Fitzwilliam propose to Elizabeth? He is a younger son (albeit of an earl) and 'Younger sons cannot marry where they like'. What, Elizabeth tartly wonders, is the 'usual price of an Earl's younger son . . . fifty thousand pounds'?

2/18 Why does Elizabeth spend six weeks at Hunsford? Visits at this period were normally of several weeks, due to the time and difficulty of travelling. It would take the visitor a day or two if not more just for the journey, so weekending was not an option. Once you were there, you lived as one of the family for, as here, weeks on end. It may also be that it is expected that Charlotte will be pregnant, in which case a close woman companion would be particularly welcome. In fact, she is not pregnant when Lizzy visits and it is only at the end of the book that we hear about the future infant olive-branch.

2/19 *When is Lydia's birthday?* In June. She 'crosses into sixteen' at Brighton.

2/20 *What is the original purpose of Elizabeth's journey north with the Gardiners?* To tour the Lakes. We know, from her earlier allusion to Gilpin's treatise on landscape, that she has read the standard guides to the 'picturesque'. She intends to see 'all the celebrated beauties of Matlock, Chatsworth, Dovedale, or the Peak'. And Pemberley—but only on the understanding that the Darcy family is not in residence.

2/21 *What bond forges an immediate friendship between the aristo-cratic Darcy and the mercantile Mr Gardiner?* Angling. There are trout in the stream which runs through the Pemberley grounds. Mr Gardiner, presumably, fishes along the Thames. Darcy offers to supply him with some tackle.

2/22 *Who is said to have 'tolerable' teeth, and by whom?* This is Miss Bingley's catty remark about Elizabeth's attractions. It goes down badly with Darcy. The remark gives one some insight into the standards of dental beauty (and hygiene, perhaps) at the period. It is not a remark one would make, even cattily, today.

2/23 *What is Mr Bennet's response, on learning of Wickham's elopement with his daughter?* He does not speak a word 'for full ten minutes'.

2/24 *What is 'peculiar' in the engagement of Anne de Bourgh to Fitzwilliam Darcy?* The fact that the principals seem not to have agreed to it. Their respective mothers (sisters) planned it while the children were 'in their cradles'. The detail is interesting. If they are the same age, Anne de Bourgh must be around 28: long in the tooth by the standards of the novel. So why has Darcy let the situation linger on? Has Lady Catherine never in fact dared to tell him her plans?

2/25 *Which of the Bennet sisters is destined to stay at home, unmarried, and care for her parents?* Mary. She has the consolation of her father's library and the piano. She is not, we understand, as 'beautiful' as her sisters. At the end of the book, we learn that Mary indeed remains at home, drawn much more into her mother's company. Jane Austen could not, however, resist mentally marrying her off, and told her family that eventually Mary married one of Uncle Philips's clerks, and was considered the intellectual star of Meryton.

Level Three

3/1 *Who informs Mrs Bennet that Netherfield Park is to be let, and what more do we learn of the lady subsequently in the narrative?* Mrs Long. She has a friendly relation with Mrs Bennet as a fellow spy on the lookout for eligible rich males. She is also, with two unmarried nieces, something of a rival in the marriageable male market. Mrs Long is 'a selfish, hypocritical woman, and I have no opinion of her' according to Mrs Bennet, in one of her more testy moments. She is evidently not rich. She does not keep a carriage and comes to the Meryton ball in a hack chaise. Later, the proud mother of a prosperously married daughter, Mrs Bennet's opinion mellows: 'I do think Mrs Long is as good a creature as ever lived—and her nieces are very pretty behaved girls, and not at all handsome: I like them prodigiously.' Piece by piece, we put together less a picture than a sketch—but a sketch with sharp lines.

3/2 *What should we read into the fact that Lydia is both the youngest and the tallest of the Bennet girls?* She has coarse vitality. Lydia is 'a stout, well-grown girl of fifteen', possessed of 'high animal spirits', we learn. This would seem to be a euphemism for sexual appetite. Lydia, who is prepared to make her own destiny, in defiance of the decencies of middle-class life, would be the heroine of a twenty-first-century novel.

3/3 *Why is Lizzy Mr Bennet's favourite and Mary his least favourite daughter?* Lizzy is 'quick', has inherited his caustic humour, and amuses him. She is witty—but not learned. Mary has presumed to set up as a bluestocking. 'You are', her father sneers at her, 'a young lady of deep reflection I know, and read great books, and make extracts'. The implication is that she has dulled herself (and lost much of her femininity) by book study. As Elizabeth explains (to a haughty Lady Catherine) the Bennet girls are largely self-educated. Teachers have been brought in, where necessary. But they have few accomplishments. Neither Jane nor Elizabeth (who has learned to play the pianoforte) has taught their younger sisters. A contemporary *Pride and Prejudice* would, perhaps, see Mary (named, perhaps, after Mary Wollstonecraft) as the most interesting of the Bennet girls. She does not interest her siblings at Longbourn. One can create a plausible and rather sad scenario: little Mary realized in her infancy that Papa liked 'Clever People Who Read Books' and desperately tried to endear herself to him by doing likewise—but as she has no quickness and sense of humour, all she becomes is pedantic and gets mocked by him instead of praised.

3/4 *What is Mrs Bennet's characteristic indisposition, and what do we deduce from it?* 'Nerves'. Neurosis would be the modern equivalent. She uses her nervousness as a means of tyrannizing over her family. One must also wonder how much Mr Bennet's sub-acid scorn has driven her neurotic. Is she a (verbally) battered wife?

3/5 *Why has Mr Bingley, who has been living in London, chosen to take a house in rural Hertfordshire?* It is, as the novel starts, autumn. Bingley, newly rich, intends to learn how to hunt and (with Darcy's tuition) acquire the necessary skills for living in a large country establishment. As one of his sisters indicates, he plans to buy a country house of his own. There is the added attraction of 'pleasant girls' in the area. Darcy will also be able to advise him on choosing a suitable wife. Darcy, of course, will not be tempted. Later in the narrative he observes that lack of 'connection' (in Jane Bennet) means much less to Bingley than it would for him—custodian as he (Darcy) is of a noble pedigree.

3/6 *How much annual income does Longbourn credit the eligible Mr Bingley with having, and where does it come from?* Mrs Bennet initially estimates Bingley as worth £4,000 or £5,000 a year. His is new money, and is probably still streaming in from whatever trade his family has prospered in. The Bingley ladies are endowed with £20,000 apiece. They have been educated 'in one of the first private seminaries in town'—London, that is, although the family originates in the north of England. They have come south to shake off the taint of trade. What trade? Most likely Yorkshire woollens—currently generating fortunes for manufacturers of military uniforms.

3/7 *Why does Miss Bingley so abuse Elizabeth (about her dirty petticoat and 'country' manners, and so on)?* She perceives that Darcy is attracted, and not just by Elizabeth's 'fine eyes'. Women have better prescience on such subjects than men.

3/8 *What are the implications of Darcy's remark, 'I cannot comprehend the neglect of a family library in such days as these'?* During the Revolutionary and Napoleonic Wars, tourism to the Continent was curtailed. A gentleman turned to his books.

3/9 *Where, cattily, does Miss Bingley suggest that the portrait of his future 'uncle and aunt Philips' (country attorney and his wife) be placed at Pemberley?* In the gallery, 'next to your great uncle the judge'. Why, one may wonder, does Darcy, if he is so grand, not have a title to his name?

3/10 *Why has Mr Collins offered his 'olive branch' to Mr Bennet?* Because Lady Catherine has 'condescended to advise him to marry as soon as he could'. Why? To protect her own daughter from the addresses of a young clergyman (she not having, like Emma Woodhouse, a Harriet Smith close to hand). It resembles a kind of castration of the harem attendant. There will be no serpents in the Eden of Rosings. Of course, it may also be that it would never cross her mind that a mere clergyman should be eligible.

3/11 *What profession was Wickham first destined for, and what do we know of his back story?* The Church, as he claims, which means that he must have gone to university (Cambridge, as we later learn). He was, by his own account, denied the promised living of Kympton with its 'excellent parsonage house'. His father, he claims, was an attorney turned steward. Miss Bingley portrays him as the son of an upper servant, not a gentleman. Darcy's father and 'old Wickham' died relatively recently. Who bought Wickham's commission? We assume it must have been Darcy, to get him out of the way.

3/12 *What fault of good manners does Mr Collins display, in introducing himself (with welcome bulletins about Lady Catherine's health) to Darcy, and how does he justify the breach?* As Elizabeth warns him, Darcy is his 'superior in consequence', and he should wait to be introduced or approached. Collins replies, reasonably enough, that clergy are above the protocols that bind the laity. He seems, for all his fatuity, to be making a good point.

3/13 *Why does Elizabeth take such a tender interest in Jane's marriage affairs, and so little in those of her younger sisters?* It is presumably her hope to live with Jane, should they both be unlucky and enter mature spinsterhood together.

3/14 *Why does Lady Catherine disapprove of entails?* Because the entail is a legal instrument for removing 'estates from the female line'.

3/15 *What does Darcy mean by his remark to Elizabeth (which 'surprises' her), 'You cannot have been always at Longbourn'?* He evidently ascribes an unprovincial sophistication to her which can only have come from travel and mixing in metropolitan society. He is wrong.

3/16 *Where and when (and how) did Wickham make his attempt on Georgiana?* At Ramsgate, the previous summer. He persuaded her to elope with him, despite the two manservants sent to accompany her, and her chaperone, Mrs Younge.

3/17 *What do we know of Mary King?* She has £10,000 and is, as Lydia says, 'a nasty little freckled thing'. After being jilted by Wickham, she goes off to her 'uncle at Liverpool'.

3/18 *What may we read into the university background of some of the novel's main characters?* If Wickham was at Cambridge, then Darcy was too, which is why he sees Wickham's dissolute lifestyle at first hand, and perceives that he is not fit to become a parson. On the other hand, Mr Collins was presumably at Oxford, as he has never come across Darcy before.

3/19 *What characterizes Lydia's letters to Kitty, from Brighton?* They have too many 'lines under the words to be made public'.

3/20 *What is the sagacious Mary's response, on learning of Lydia's running away?* 'This useful lesson; that loss of virtue in a female is irretrievable'. The Augustan truism ('When lovely lady stoops to folly') reduces Elizabeth to speechless exasperation.

3/21 *Why does Wickham accept the surprisingly modest settlement of £100 p.a. from Mr Bennet?* It is a perplexingly small sum (as Mr B. says, 'Wickham's a fool if he takes her with a farthing less than ten thousand pounds'). One assumes that it is a token, indicative of family assent, a tacit condoning of their elopement, and possibly, too, Wickham calculates it worthwhile to have a steady income of £100 p.a., even if this is not the wealth he has dedicated his career to acquiring. Also, he must realize by now that Mr Bennet cannot afford to give his daughters a fortune and he may as well accept the bird in the hand—more so since Darcy will pay £1,000-plus to clear his debts as well as settling another £1,000 on Lydia herself, and buying a commission in the regulars for Wickham. Wickham may well be thinking cynically of abandoning Lydia at some future date and disappearing into military life elsewhere; or perhaps she might die in childbed. Like Frank Churchill, he may be hoping for any and every possibility to get out of a tight scrape.

3/22 *Where does Wickham (with Darcy's money) get his commission in the 'regulars'?* In General ——'s regiment, quartered far away in the North (Newcastle, we later learn). The remoteness was, presumably, one of the conditions insisted on by Darcy. Lydia's saying she may be out of touch for three years suggests the regiment is due for service overseas.

3/23 *How does Elizabeth learn that Darcy was at the wedding of Lydia and Wickham?* Lydia 'accidentally' (surely not) lets the 'secret' slip. Elizabeth immediately writes to her aunt, 'to request an explanation'. Why should Darcy have been there, one may ask—unless it was with the intention that the information should get back to Longbourn? Or perhaps, it was to ensure that Wickham turned up? Was he the best man? Or a signing witness to the ceremony?

3/24 *Does Lydia know about the financial assistance which Darcy has made? Is she, that is to say, an accomplice in this extortion?* Probably yes.

3/25 *Why does Mrs Bennet assume that Elizabeth and Darcy will be married by 'special licence'?* It would be quite possible for them to marry in the normal fashion, by having the banns called three Sundays running in each of their respective parish churches (Pemberley and Meryton). Mrs Bennet is keen on a special licence because it was considered the smart thing to do.

Level Four

4/1 How long have Mr and Mrs Bennet been married (an easy question), and why on earth did he marry her (the most difficult question in the novel)? 'Three and twenty years'. Although the rapid production of children was normal at this period (even if not everywhere in Jane Austen's fiction), for him to have had five daughters in seven years is the clue, perhaps, to why he should have married such an intellectually inadequate partner. Sex. And, latterly, he was driven to propagation in order to produce the male heir who would keep Longbourn estate from his obnoxious cousin. Make love in haste, repent in leisure, would seem the moral to be drawn from Mr Bennet's choice of wife. Later in the narrative, Elizabeth's view on her father confirms this analysis. He was captivated in his headstrong younger years by Miss Gardiner's (then) youth and beauty, and her 'appearance of good humour'. She also brought a useful dowry (around £5,000) to the marriage. He did not, before leaping into matrimony, pay sufficient attention to her 'weak understanding and illiberal mind'. In his late marital life, Mr Bennet retires to his study and a Shandyan mode of existence. Very late in the novel we are told that 'for many years after Lydia's birth' he had been certain he would produce a male heir, who would cut off the entail, but that eventually (with Mrs Bennet's menopause, presumably, or perhaps some gynaecological damage after the rapid production of so many offspring) this hope was 'despaired of'.

4/2 What can we reconstruct of Mr and Mrs Bennet's 'back story'? We learn, through Mr Collins's letter, of a 'disagreement subsisting' between Mr Bennet and his cousin. We learn later that the cousin was 'illiterate and miserly'. Legally minded critics have sorted out this family history as follows: Mr Bennet and Mr Collins senior were first cousins, the sons of two sisters, and the Longbourn estate belonged to their maternal grandfather or uncle. He, having no son of his own, made a settlement of the estate on his daughters' or sisters' male offspring: on Mr Bennet for life with the remainder to his son; failing a Bennet son, the male inheritance would revert to Mr Collins senior and so to his son, the Revd William Collins. He has been brought up in another part of the country.

Although scholarly, Mr Bennet does not seem to be a university man. He is also notably solitary, verging on misanthropic. Mrs Bennet's father was a prosperous attorney in Meryton. Mrs Bennet's sister married the lawyer's clerk, Mr Philips. She has a brother settled in London in 'a respectable line of trade' (in her private thoughts, Elizabeth euphemizes it as 'in business'). Mr Gardiner is a merchant, presumably, in the import and export trade. We learn that he lives (to the contemptuous amusement of the Bingley ladies) 'somewhere near Cheapside'. Enough said.

4/3 *Why does Mr Bennet tease and tantalize his wife so?* Because, in his way, he is a domestic tyrant. Teasing also seems the means by which he controls his irritation at her stupidity (and his own stupidity for having married her).

4/4 *When, at the Meryton ball that brings the principals together, Darcy makes his disagreeable remark that 'She is tolerable; but not handsome enough to tempt* me; *and I am in no humour at present to give consequence to young ladies who are slighted by other men', he is overheard by Elizabeth (and, as we apprehend, her mother). Does he mean to be overheard? Should we perhaps assume the music momentarily stopped? Is he, perhaps, a little deaf?* Pitching one's voice in order to be overheard was, evidently, something of a social skill in the period. Mrs Bennet does it very effectively to embarrass Darcy, later in the narrative. It is clear that someone has been gossiping maliciously about Elizabeth. She has not been slighted by other men. Later in the narrative we learn that Darcy is also under the misapprehension that Elizabeth, alone of the Bennet girls, has travelled.

4/5 *In conversation with Charlotte (who was at the Meryton ball),* *an exasperated Elizabeth says that Jane 'danced four dances with [Bingley]'. As the eagle-eyed Mrs Bennet notes (frequently), it was two dances only. What do we read into the error?* The answer may lie in the conventions of the ballroom at this time. It would seem that each dance, as such, was in two parts—the two first, two second, two third, etc. This would mean you danced twice, which totalled four dances. It could, clearly, create some numerical confusion.

4/6 *Why does Darcy, at the Netherfield ball, resolve to break up the romance between Bingley and Jane?* His motives are never clear, other than that it is his 'pride' which is at fault (as unsatisfactory in its way as Shylock's 'It is my humour'). He claims, later, that he presumed there was no love on Jane's side, being persuaded by the 'serenity' of her demeanour.

4/7 *Why does Mr Collins ask Mrs Bennet's permission to propose to Elizabeth, but not Mr Bennet's? And why, three days later, does he propose to Charlotte without consulting either of the young lady's parents?* As he earlier explained to Elizabeth, he is a clergyman and can break some rules. Also, at 27, Charlotte is, at least, independent. Most plausibly, given the nature of the gentleman, Mr Collins gets Charlotte's agreement before asking her parents, because he did it the other way round with Mrs Bennet and Lizzy, and then got thoroughly snubbed. He does not intend to be snubbed a second time.

4/8 *Why does not Mr Bennet encourage his heir, Mr Collins, in his addresses to his eligible daughters? If not Lizzy (whom he does not want to lose) then Mary?* An added reason is that we are specifically told that Mary likes Mr Collins (even though she thinks he's not as clever as herself)—unlike her sister, who instinctively dislikes the clergyman. Mr Bennet seems to be incorrigibly selfish. After he dies his womenfolk will be left near destitute, and evicted from their home. It seems an eventuality that does not disturb his equanimity. As Mrs Bennet says to her daughters, 'I do not know who is to maintain you when your father is dead'. Who, one wonders, is to maintain her?

4/9 *Who does Darcy bring to Rosings with him, and what plot details may we weave around it?* He brings his cousin, Colonel Fitzwilliam, 'about thirty, not handsome, but in person and address most truly the gentleman'. Apparently misanthropic, Darcy seems strangely averse to solitude (at least, when visits to his formidable aunt are concerned). Yet he obviously has not confided in his cousin his growing attraction towards Elizabeth— since the Colonel himself clearly considers proposing, before deciding against it, on grounds of financial prudence.

4/10 *When Darcy lists as the disqualifications of Elizabeth's family the 'want of propriety' of her mother and younger sisters and 'occasionally . . . your father', what is he thinking of?* Mr Bennet's partiality for Wickham: of which we see little evidence. But George Wickham obviously has the knack of winning over older men—as he did with Darcy's father.

4/11 *How many professions and occupations has Wickham had?* He was sent to Cambridge and graduated, after which he inherited a £1,000 bequest from Mr Darcy senior. He received a further £3,000 from Darcy on his giving up any claim to the Kympton living. Wickham subsequently went into the law, but spent his pupillage in dissipation. After his unsuccessful attempt to elope with the 15-year-old Georgiana Darcy (attracted by her £30,000 fortune), he bought himself, or was bought, a commission in the militia, which is where the novel joins him. When plans for marriage with the ten-thousand-pounder Mary King fail, he turns, at last, to honest work. Wickham, as a professional man, probably has more strings to his bow than any other character in Jane Austen.

4/12 *What are the salient features of Pemberley that so delight the judicious Elizabeth Bennet?* It has no 'artificial appearance . . . She had never seen a place for which nature had done more, or where natural beauty had been so little counteracted by an awkward taste'. It has 'less of splendour' but more 'real elegance' than Rosings. Elizabeth is already thinking like an owner.

4/13 *Why* does *Wickham elope with Lydia?* This is one of the great mysteries of the plot. He is an adventurer, but Lydia is no prize. Nor, one imagines, would she deny her physical attractions to such a plausible wooer. Moreover, there are risks for him: as Mr Gardiner points out, Lydia is 'by no means unprotected or friendless'. He has, we are guardedly told, already seduced a number of girls in Meryton—tradesmen's, not gentlemen's, daughters, we are delicately instructed. Why would someone so normally calculating and self-interested prejudice his military career with this act? (Colonel Forster would, by army regulation, have to approve a junior officer's marriage; and Lydia was, in any case, his ward—staying with Mrs Forster, an accomplice to the elopement.) Harriet Forster's role is mysterious—but certainly culpable. Given the age of Mr Bennet (and the civilian profession of Mr Gardiner), if it comes to duels, Wickham might find himself taking the field against his own commanding officer. He has, apparently, not even confided his intentions to his bride. Lydia evidently thinks they are going to Gretna Green, as she tells Harriet. Instead, they take lodgings in London, helped by Mrs Younge, who was dismissed (handsomely paid off) for conspiring to help Georgiana elope with Wickham. She now has a house in Edward Street, in the West End of London. Wickham and Lydia call on her there, but she has no room for them, so Wickham goes into lodgings in the parish of St Clement's, and the Gardiners take Lydia back to Gracechurch Street with them. There is nice symbolism in Lydia's final instruction to Harriet, 'tell Sally to mend a great slit in my worked muslin gown'. Some slits, once opened, can never be mended. The only thing, as Elizabeth tells Darcy, that can 'tempt' Wickham is Lydia's virginity, and once he has that, 'she is lost for ever': Wickham presumably wins that prize before marriage.

Mr Bennet and Colonel Forster enquire at the inns along the lovers' presumed travel route from Brighton to Gretna Green via London (particularly in Barnet and Hatfield). We may assume that one of the questions they ask the innkeepers is 'did the couple share a room, and under what name?' Lydia, none the less, has admirable pluck. She refuses to leave Wickham, even after it is clear that they are not on their way to Scotland. She is, presumably, at this stage a mistress (for all her later pride in being a respectably married woman) and possibly even pregnant. Her gay theory is 'she was sure they should be married some time or other, and it did not much signify when'. When Edward Gardiner catches up with the couple (thanks to Darcy) he says, 'they are not married, nor can I find there was any intention of being so'.

So, why did Wickham marry her? Given his threat to leave her, and 'make his fortune by marriage, in some other country' one assumes that blackmail has been his motive all along. Given Wickham's cunning, we must assume that he intended to blackmail either Mr Gardiner or—if he had caught wind, as he probably did, of Darcy's feelings for Elizabeth—his previous victim. Darcy astutely guesses the connection with Mrs Younge and bribes her for the information. One of the conditions laid on the seducer is that Wickham shall, until the wedding, live in separate lodgings, in St Clements. And that the banns be called there. Even so, Mr Collins will later accuse Mr B. of being an encourager of vice, for receiving his married daughter when 'their living together before the marriage took place, should be so generally known'. How was it generally known?

4/14 *Why, at Pemberley, does Elizabeth confide Lydia's elopement to Darcy?* She gives the unconvincing reason that 'it cannot be concealed from anyone'. The truth is that she is looking for a strong man—someone to fill the hole so prominently left by Mr Bennet, who comes out very badly from this section of the narrative.

4/15 *How does Mr Collins learn of the elopement, and what does he do with his information?* He receives 'a letter from Hertfordshire'. From Lady Lucas, of course. He dutifully passes the scandal on to Lady Catherine. At this point, or soon after, someone must also tell the august patroness that her nephew has an interest in Elizabeth. Charlotte is obviously the communication link between Hertfordshire and Kent and back again.

4/16 *What can we deduce about Wickham's conduct during his three months at Brighton, leading up to the elopement?* He ran up debts, of a thousand pounds or more. How, one wonders. He must have gamed wildly, to lose that much—or have dissipated himself magnificently. Given the short period he must have lived like Byron, Beau Brummel, and the Prince Regent rolled into one.

4/17 *Why, after he has married Lydia, is Elizabeth so friendly and amicable with Wickham?* Their last exchange is his kissing her hand, and her smiling at him, good-humouredly. We should not assume that he is irresistible. Lizzy has evidently realized that it is better not to have an open break in the family, much as she despises her new brother-in-law. There has been enough scandal.

4/18 *In their post-proposal intimate conversations, Bingley tells Jane (who tells Elizabeth) 'that he was totally ignorant of my being in town last spring'. Is this plausible?* No. If their paths had not crossed, over three months, is it likely that her name, and some discussion of Longbourn, would never have come up? Jane hazards, 'it must have been his sister's doing' (Jane's sister-in-law to be). The two ladies were, of course, in correspondence when Jane was in Gracechurch Street—and even exchanged visits. Darcy admits that *he* knew that Jane was in London, and kept Bingley in the dark. He may also have warned off Caroline. It is a murky little side-plot. And yet, we are told, when Bingley returned to London in November 'he really loved' Jane. As in some other episodes, Bingley emerges as either very much duped by trusted friends, or a virtual simpleton. Or both.

4/19 *Who gave Lady Catherine de Bourgh the 'report of an alarming nature' that not only was Jane to marry Bingley, but that 'Miss Elizabeth Bennet, would, in all likelihood, be soon afterwards united to my own nephew, Mr Darcy'?* This is a great mystery, more so since the presumption at Longbourn (and presumably at Meryton) is that the two young people dislike each other. Elizabeth's deduction is unconvincing—namely that it is a simple association of ideas, with the Jane and Bingley union imminent.

Mr Bennet assumes it must be 'some of the good-natured, gossiping Lucases'. But the informant must, logically, be Charlotte—whether from benign or malicious motives is debatable. We are later told that Charlotte 'really' rejoices in the match. The word 'really' may be loaded.

4/20 *Lady Catherine de Bourgh boasts to Elizabeth that her daughter and Darcy are descended 'on the maternal side, from the same noble line; and, on the father's, from respectable, and ancient, though untitled families.' With the other information that Darcy's cousin Colonel Fitzwilliam is the son of an earl, what kind of family tree can one construct from this?* The old Earl of Somewhere, family name Fitzwilliam, had two sisters, Lady Catherine and Lady Anne. They, as we know, marry Sir Lewis de Bourgh and the rich Mr Darcy, producing respectively Miss Anne de Bourgh and Fitzwilliam Darcy. The old earl also marries, has a son—the present or future earl—and a younger son, Colonel Fitzwilliam. This officer is therefore cousin to Mr Fitzwilliam Darcy and nephew to Lady Catherine de Bourgh.

4/21 *It is conventionally observed that Miss Austen never shows two gentlemen in conversation together without a lady present. Is there any exception to this rule of her fictional universe?* After their day's shooting, when Bingley intends to ask for Jane's hand, we are told that he and Mr Bennet spend the morning together: 'The latter [i.e. the suitor] was much more agreeable than his companion [the father] expected. There was nothing of presumption or folly in Bingley, that could provoke his ridicule, or disgust him into silence; and he [Mr Bennet] was more communicative, and less eccentric that the other had ever seen him.' This pleasant intercourse, and the manly conversation, cannot have been overheard, or observed, by any lady. It will be noted, of course, that the narrator does not actually *show* the conversation, but merely tells the reader its content.

4/22 *When, Jane asks Elizabeth, did Elizabeth begin to love Darcy? Elizabeth replies: 'I believe it must date from my first seeing his* *beautiful grounds at Pemberley.' Is this ironic, or is she really as affected by real estate as the remark might imply?* It is hard to say. But it seems, in Derbyshire, she understood him and his 'pride' better.

4/23 *Mr Bennet says, some weeks after Lydia's wedding and on learning that Darcy had paid over the necessary bribes: 'And so Darcy did everything ... Had it been your uncle's [Gardiner's] doing, I must and would have paid him.' Would he?* If he has left it this long, and not made enquiry on the matter (and assuming his brother-in-law has not lied to him) the expectation is that his indolence would have solved the problem in the usual way. He would not.

4/24 *Why is the proud, cultivated and snobbish Darcy the 'inseparable' friend of Bingley, a man of limited intelligence and no firmness of mind?* One assumes that Darcy likes servility. Bingley invariably does what his friend (or failing that, his sister) tells him. How did the two young men become acquainted? It could not, given the difference of age, have been at Cambridge. It may well have been a school friendship, the young Bingley being a fag, or whatever, to Darcy at Eton, perhaps, establishing a kind of mentor relationship between them.

4/25 *Why does Bingley (and his future wife) so readily forgive Darcy for keeping from him, the previous winter, the fact that Jane was in London—causing huge pain to the lady?* Because he is Fitzwilliam Darcy, and not answerable to any one.

Northanger Abbey

Level One

1/1 *What is Mr Morland's profession? How well off is he? What is the source of his wealth?* Mr Morland is a country clergyman with two good livings (one of which, worth £400 a year, he plans to give to his eldest son, James). He also has 'independent' wealth (in land, and the 'funds'—Isabella's fantasies magnify this wealth later in the narrative). He is sufficiently 'warm' to send his sons to school and university but is not, with such a large family, able (or inclined) to afford a governess for his daughters.

1/2 *How many children do the Revd Mr and Mrs Morland have? How many of their Christian names do we know?* The Morlands have ten children. Catherine is 17 at the beginning of the narrative proper, 18 when she gets married. She has three older brothers. The eldest Morland son, at a putative 22, is James, the heir. Richard is a putative 20. A third son, unnamed, must be about 18. Early in the narrative Sarah ('Sally') is identified, aged 16. When Catherine returns to Fullerton at the end of the novel, we are briefly introduced to the two youngest of the family, George, aged 6, and Harriet who is just 4. There are three unnamed boys, between Sally and George. How do we know they are boys? Because they are away at school—an educational advantage denied the Morland girls.

1/3 *What boisterous games does Catherine play as a girl?* Cricket and baseball. She also rides horses and, we are told, runs about the countryside. The influence of three older brothers, presumably. Had they been sisters it would have been dolls and gardening. The reference to both these manly sports has intrigued commentators. One ingenious Janeite has speculated that the author's interest in cricket was stimulated by the local, all-conquering, Hambledon eleven and that 'We must assume that

Jane was a Hampshire supporter'. 'Baseball' was, in the 1780s, more like 'rounders' than what the fans watch nowadays at Dodger Stadium.

1/4 *How many children do the rich Allens have?* None. He is, we gather from a number of references, a man of rather retiring tastes: she is a fashion-mad wife. They have no children, which may suggest that Mrs Allen's addiction to fashionable dress is a displacement neurosis, compounded by the boredom of living in the country.

1/5 *How much money does Mr Morland give Catherine as her Bath allowance? What do we learn that she spends it on?* Mr Morland gives his daughter ten guineas. In the course of the novel we learn that Catherine spends her modest allowance on, *inter alia*: a sprigged muslin gown, a straw bonnet, and a new writing desk (the latter indicating a promising seriousness and indifference to the fashions which obsess Mrs Allen and Miss Thorpe).

1/6 *How old is Henry Tilney?* 'He seemed to be about four or five and twenty.' At the end of the novel we learn he is 25 at this point. In a marriage market, like Bath, these age calibrations are vital.

1/7 *What is Henry's profession, and how does Catherine learn of it?* He is a clergyman, but she does not learn this until later, after Mr Allen has made the guardian's discreet enquiries in the Lower Rooms. Mrs Allen learns a bit more about the wealthiness of the Tilneys from Mrs Hughes when they are in the Pump Room and walking in the Crescent, some days later.

Clerics did not, at this period, have to wear clerical garb. See, for example, *Mansfield Park*, where Mary Crawford reminds herself that Edmund can look like any other young landed gent—'there is no distinction of dress nowadays'. Latitudinarian in his theology and mufti in his dress, Henry's vocation does not prevent him dancing or hunting; at home in Woodston he is as much squire as parson. In Bath he is indistinguishable from other young gentlemen on the prowl for wives.

1/8 *How much older than Catherine is 'Miss Thorpe' (that is, Isabella)?* Isabella is in her fourth (desperate) season as an unmarried woman at Bath. She is, presumably, 21; four years ahead of Catherine; a husband-hunter on the cusp of spinsterdom.

1/9 *What is the first, and what the second, novel Catherine and Isabella read together?* Respectively, *The Mysteries of Udolpho* and *The Italian*. Both of these works by Mrs Radcliffe were hot off the press—novels of 1796 and 1797 respectively. It is not clear that Catherine does read *The Italian* (Isabella has already done so). After a week, life at Bath becomes very busy for the young women.

1/10 *How much did John Thorpe pay Freeman, of Christ Church, for his gig?* Fifty guineas. Around five times what Mr Morland gave Catherine as six weeks' allowance, and Sir Thomas Bertram gives Fanny Price as pocket money for her two months' punitive sojourn in Portsmouth. Did he squander this much of his mother's scarce wealth? Given what we know of John's grandiosity, he could be boasting, to display how rich he is: fifty guineas means nothing to *him*.

1/11 *Where are James and John students?* Oxford; we don't know the college. We do, however, know two colleges where they are not: Oriel and Christ Church. How? Because John Thorpe identifies his friend Freeman as being at the second, and Jackson at the first. Sam Fletcher, we may assume, is of the same college (whichever) as James and John.

1/12 *In Bath, after the Thursday evening ball, Catherine is exultant: 'her spirits danced within her, as she danced in her chair all the way home.' What chair is this?* A 'Bath chair' or 'sedan chair', presumably. The sedan chair was carried on shafts by two chairmen. As the *Encyclopaedia Britannica* puts it, the Bath chair was a 'chair on wheels intended for use by ladies and invalids. It was devised by James Heath, about 1750. For the next three-quarters of a century it rivalled the sedan chair and ultimately superseded it as a form of conveyance in Great Britain. The most common variety was supported on two wheels joined by an axle beneath the seat, with a small pivoting wheel in front.' Catherine, of course, is not an invalid.

1/13 *What is Miss Tilney's first name?* We learn from an unguarded comment of Henry's that it is Eleanor (the name was wildly fashionable, from Gottfried Bürger's much translated ballad about a lover who returns from the dead to reclaim his bride).

1/14 *What aspect of Catherine's walk does General Tilney particularly admire?* Her 'elasticity'. The material 'elastic' was not, in fact, invented until 1823 and in 1798 the compliment would not have the odd associations it now carries. The implication here would be that Catherine's gait is springy, lithe, light-footed.

1/15 *Where did Henry go to university?* Oxford. But he in no way resembles his fellow Oxonian, Thorpe.

1/16 *What is Isabella Thorpe's family nickname?* Belle.

1/17 *What profession is James intended for?* The Church. Isabella may have been slightly self-deluded on this issue, expecting her future husband will be something grander than a country parson.

1/18 *In what service is Frederick Tilney a captain?* The army. His regiment is the 12th Light Dragoons (that is, mounted infantry— they would use their horses until engaged in battle).

1/19 *Is Captain Frederick the elder, or younger brother?* Elder.

1/20 *What was Northanger Abbey originally?* Once a richly endowed convent, it has belonged to ancestors of the Tilneys since the Dissolution (presumably through the female line, hence the initial on the old chest is not 'T'). Gothic in style (Austen applies the term to architecture, but never to fiction), the pile was partly modernized by General Tilney's father. In its modern condition it requires scores of servants, gardeners, and grooms to keep it running. Hence, perhaps, its proprietor's avarice.

1/21 *What does Catherine realize she has found in the black cabinet?* A laundry list, and bills for hair-powder, shoe-string, a breeches-ball (clothes cleaner), and a farrier's bill for the poulticing of a 'chesnut [*sic*] mare'.

1/22 *Does Henry have a butler at Woodston?* No, just an old housekeeper.

1/23 *What are the 'friends of Henry's solitude' at Woodston?* Not his curate, but 'a large Newfoundland puppy and two or three terriers'.

1/24 *What pretext does the General give for throwing Catherine out of Northanger Abbey, with a bare eight hours' notice and no servant?* 'An engagement' to Lord Longtown, near Hereford.

1/25 *Who has disabused the General as to Catherine's prospects?* John Thorpe. Over the billiard table, presumably.

Level Two

2/1 *When, and why, does Catherine give up her tomboy pursuits?* Precisely at 15, with the onset of menstruation. Vigorous exercise would, thereafter, be thought inadvisable. None the less, there are a number of references in the text to Catherine's precipitately 'running' where more genteel young ladies would walk. She probably knows more about equine management than John Thorpe, and could throw a cricket ball farther than his pudgy arm—did decorum allow.

2/2 *Where is Catherine brought up? What do we know of the place?* Catherine, as best we can make out, has passed her whole life up to the age of 17 at the village of Fullerton in Wiltshire. It is stultifyingly small. Mr Allen owns most of the property in the vicinity (his house is visible from the Morlands' parsonage), and the Allen household is the only one within walking distance for Catherine. Fullerton is around nine miles from Salisbury, which is where Catherine will do her serious shopping. Apart from the Allens, some forty families—respectable families, that is—are resident within a ten-mile visiting/dining radius of the Morlands.

2/3 *What happy accident takes Catherine to Bath?* Mr Allen's 'gouty disposition'. Mrs Allen, we are told, is 'fond' of Catherine. More importantly, the role of chaperone will give her an excuse— which she would otherwise not have—of attending 'public assemblies' (that is, dances) and showing off her newly purchased finery. Mr Allen's gout is a pretext to get away from the boredom of winter in Fullerton. On their part, with three daughters to dispose of, seven boys to educate, and the heir, James, to provide for, the Morlands are not unwilling to hurl 17-year-old Catherine into the marriage market. One down, nine to go, will be going through their fond, but realistic, parental minds.

2/4 *How do Mrs Allen and Mrs Thorpe recognize each other?* They were at school together. They have since met once, fifteen years ago, which explains how Mrs Thorpe knows her school friend's married name. It is a tribute to her having avoided the rigours of childbearing that Mrs Allen, unlike Mrs Thorpe, is still recognizable as the schoolgirl she once was.

2/5 *What do we know of Henry's complexion, and what does it mean?* He has 'brown skin, with dark eyes, and rather dark hair'. Fair and pallid complexions were more fashionable. Henry's colour suggests an outdoor life. His brother, Captain Frederick Tilney, has a 'florid' complexion suggestive of a dissipated mode of life his brother avoids.

2/6 *What colour dress (as Mrs Allen's needle-sharp eye notes) does Miss Tilney 'always wear'?* White. It means that the Tilneys have a full complement of servants. She need not wear clothes more than once before they are laundered. In *Mansfield Park*, Mrs Norris believes in turning away maids who presume to wear white—that colour is above their station in life.

2/7 *How does John Thorpe come to have known General Tilney?* They have met at the Bedford Coffee House in Covent Garden (London's theatre and red-light area; parts of which are neither a proper resort for a serving general nor an Oxford undergraduate during term time). And they have played billiards together. The General is an excellent player, John reports (he may not be entirely reliable—even on areas where he likes to mis-spend his youth).

2/8 *Who does John Thorpe take on the jaunt to Clifton, when Catherine obstinately refuses?* His younger sister, Maria (whose ankles, presumably, are no shame to the family).

2/9 *Who gave Catherine a lecture on fashion and when?* Her great-aunt, the Christmas before. This is interesting as being one of the very few occasions in Jane Austen's fiction in which we meet generations older than parents. It is suggested this is probably because the novelist herself never knew her grandparents, all of whom had died before she was born.

2/10 *What is Catherine's first response on being invited to Northanger Abbey?* She writes home for permission from her parents.

2/11 *Who says, 'after all that romancers may say, there is no doing without money'?* Isabella Thorpe, gold-digger that she is.

2/12 *For what does the General rebuke Frederick on the day the rest of the family leave Bath?* Being late for breakfast.

2/13 *By what transportation does Catherine go from Bath to Northanger Abbey?* On the first leg, a slow, pompous post-chaise-and-four (in the company of Eleanor and her maid). On the second, merrier leg, with Henry in his two-person curricle (that is, driver and passenger). The curricle enables Catherine to have a happy private chat with Henry.

2/14 *Where is Henry's house, and living? What kind of house is it?* Woodston, twenty miles from Northanger Abbey. The parsonage is new, and of stone construction.

2/15 *Who has the gift of Woodston?* It is a family living.

2/16 *How long ago did Mrs Tilney die, and of what?* She died when Eleanor was 13, nine years before, of a 'bilious fever'.

2/17 *What, when she finally effects an entrance, does Catherine find in the 'mysterious apartment'?* 'A handsome dimity bed ... a bright Bath stove, mahogany wardrobes and neatly-painted chairs'. The room was renovated by the General's father.

2/18 *Since Lady Fraser is not in the neighbourhood and a big dinner at Northanger is therefore out of the question, what does General Tilney suggest?* That they dine at Woodston. His motive, one assumes, is to show off Henry's rectory to Catherine, as a bait for her as an heiress (as he supposes). Jane Austen probably wants readers to 'see' Woodston so that they can envisage the domestic joys which (after many trials) await our heroine.

2/19 *How long has Catherine been at Northanger Abbey when General Tilney goes on his fateful visit to London for a week?* Between three and four weeks.

2/20 *Why has Catherine, even before the General's wrathful return, suggested that she should, perhaps, leave?* She will be intruding, she says, and presuming on the privileges of a guest. One deduces that the Morlands have brought their children up to be excessively well mannered. They must, above all, not overstay a welcome and appear like greedy hangers-on.

2/21 *What are Catherine's first thoughts when Eleanor disturbs her in her bedroom on Saturday night, 'on such an errand! . . . Oh! how shall I tell you!'?* She immediately suspects something awful has happened to her beloved ("'Tis a messenger from Woodston!').

2/22 *In what sort of vehicle does Catherine travel back to Fullerton?* A humble hack post-chaise—hired public transport, a country taxi-service.

2/23 *How long is it before Henry appears at Fullerton to propose?* Three days. He has taken a whole day to consider his rebellious action. It is a rational decision, not hasty. He has, of course, his ('very considerable') personal fortune from his mother's 'settlements'.

2/24 *What finally makes the General agree to the marriage of Henry and Catherine, and how does he phrase his consent?* 'The marriage of his daughter with a man of fortune' (we do not learn his name, but he was the owner of the laundry list which so disappointed Catherine). The General's surly permission is that Henry is free 'to be a fool if he liked it'.

2/25 *How long do the lovers have to wait for paternal consent?* A year, making Catherine a more respectable 18.

Level Three

3/1 *We are told that Catherine's father was 'a very respectable man, though his name was Richard'. What do we make of the gibe against this harmless Christian name?* This tart sarcasm has baffled commentators. It is suggested that 'Richard' was a name against which the Austen family had an irrational prejudice, and about which it pleased them to make jokes (there are a couple of throw-away comments in Jane Austen's letters supporting this supposition). Perhaps the tradition of playing Shakespeare's Richard III as the blackest of villains darkened the name. Coming where it does, in the third sentence of the novel, this sly in-joke reminds us that Austen's most privileged readers were her own family (effectively the only readership the novel had for almost two decades).

3/2 *What is Mrs Morland's favourite novel?* It is *Sir Charles Grandison*, by Samuel Richardson. Published in 1754, it was all the rage when she was Catherine's age. The plot of the novel has some resemblance to that of *Northanger Abbey*.

3/3 *On the journey to Bath, Mrs Allen fears she has left her clogs at an inn. Why would a rich woman, fanatic about her wardrobe, wear these?* Leather overshoes, known as 'clogs', were worn in dry conditions, inside the house, carriage or sedan chair, to protect a lady's lightweight fabric shoes—hence Mrs Allen's anxiety at their possible loss.

3/4 *When Mrs Thorpe boasts about her children, how does the childless Mrs Allen console herself?* 'With the discovery, which her keen eye soon made, that the lace on Mrs Thorpe's pelisse was not half so handsome as that on her own'.

3/5 *What reasons does John Thorpe give for not bothering to read Fanny Burney's* Camilla? Burney is married to an 'emigrant', that is, a French refugee, an anti-republican, and an aristocrat. In addition to his other offences, Thorpe is, presumably, something of a Jacobin. Austen's family were firmly of the other, anti-Jacobin, party. John, who is no literary critic, is moreover of the opinion that the novel is about nothing but an old man playing on the see-saw and learning Latin. Poor Fanny Burney.

3/6 *What over the course of the novel do we learn of the Thorpes? How many of them are there at Bath and how should we picture them?* They are the relics of a lawyer at Putney, and 'not rich'. John, the eldest at 22, and his mother's favourite, is at Oxford and wasting the family's substance (hence the desperation to get the daughters married). Isabella—nicknamed, aptly, 'Belle' by her family—has the good looks. There are two other, younger, daughters. Of Anne (aged around 19) we only know that she has 'thick ankles'. Maria, two years younger than Anne, has her elder sister's looks. Edward (16?) is at Merchant Taylors' School. William (14?) is at sea, a midshipman. Mrs Thorpe has brought the girls to the Bath marriage market while the boys are safely occupied elsewhere.

3/7 *Catherine is frustratingly prevented from joining the dance at the Upper Rooms because John Thorpe absents himself in the card room. What is he doing there?* Not playing cards. Possibly drinking to give himself courage. But he then tells Catherine, with insulting stupidity, he's been delayed because of the more important business of discussing dogs and horses with some crony. He lacks a lover's smooth address.

3/8 *Why, having just arrived at Bath (to arrange accommodation for himself and his father and sister), does Henry suddenly leave, and what should we deduce from his departure?* He has returned to Woodston to take a Sunday service, declining to leave it to his curate. His conscientiousness contrasts with that of the two truanting Oxonians.

3/9 *How much money did the late Mrs Tilney (née Drummond) bring with her on marriage to the General?* As Mrs Allen ascertains, £20,000, plus £500 with which to buy wedding clothes. Mrs Allen gets this information from Mrs Hughes (a schoolfellow of Mrs Tilney and chaperone to Eleanor).

3/10 *This is a quiz. What does the slangy word mean in 1798 at Bath—when, for example, John Thorpe says that his sisters and their partners are 'the four greatest quizzes in the room'?* There is no modern equivalent. It means, roughly, 'grotesques', 'freaks', or 'oddities'.

3/11 *Who is John Thorpe's hunting companion?* Sam Fletcher. They intend to get a house together in Leicestershire 'next

season'. Let us hope Mrs Thorpe's modest exchequer can
stand it.

3/12 *What do we know of the Skinners?* Dr Skinner could be the
Allens' doctor. Last year the Skinners stayed three months at
Bath and got 'stout' (Mr Allen, we understand, could benefit
from more flesh on his bones). 'Stout' at this period did not
necessarily mean, as it does with us, 'obese', but 'healthy, sturdy'.
Bath, that is, did him good. It is, perhaps, as likely that Dr Skinner
is the *Revd* Dr Skinner—with a DD in theology; perhaps, one
might go on to speculate, the incumbent of the next parish to
Fullerton, on the other side of the Allens' estate.

3/13 *How does Mr Morland respond to James's surprising declaration that he is in love and intends to marry?* Kindly, but sensibly.
He is assured of his father's second living, which will be worth
£400 (currently, Mr Morland serves both: with advancing years,
he may expect it to be too much). James will get a similar amount
on his father's death. But Mr Morland declines to touch his
landed property or his funded money (most of which probably
only exists in Isabella's imagination). And, most shrewdly,
Mr Morland indicates that James will have to wait almost three
years before he can have the living (a bare subsistence, as Isabella
thinks). It is not bloody-mindedness. James will, like Henry
Tilney, have to wait until he is 24 or 25 before he can be ordained,
and so be financially able to marry. The young Revd Morland's
bride will herself be 24 by then. She expected immediate
marriage (she is already contemplating her wedding gown).

3/14 *What do we deduce from General Tilney's being disappointed
by the non-arrival of his 'friends' the Marquis of Longtown and
General Courteney?* For someone so preoccupied with his own
station in life, he seems to have little grand company. On the
other hand, we only observe him at home for some four weeks.
He may, perhaps, have throngs of guests over other seasons of the
year, entertaining them not in the common, but in the other,
enormous drawing-room. There are morning callers at the Abbey

while Catherine is staying there—but they are received in the breakfast room without any great ceremony.

3/15 *Why does Henry say that Captain Tilney 'must be his own master'?* Frederick is the elder brother. By primogeniture he will, in course of time, be the head of the family. He may not be gainsaid by his junior sibling, even if that sibling is a man of the cloth.

3/16 *On the trip to Northanger Abbey we are informed that Catherine has a 'new writing desk'. What may we deduce from it?* She is dutifully thinking of writing letters, and being able to do so in the drawing-room (where a locked escritoire would be left). Needless to say, a propensity for penmanship is a good moral quality in Austen's fictional world. Catherine must have bought it with money given her for clothes. Isabella, doubtless, would not have wasted her substance on a writing desk. Leave those to the schoolchildren.

3/17 *What is the first sound that awakes Catherine on the morning after the night of the storm?* 'The housemaid's folding back her window-shutters at eight'. She has also, silently, lit a fire.

3/18 *What is Eleanor Tilney's favourite walk and why?* The path through 'a thick grove of old Scotch firs'. It was her mother's favourite walk.

3/19 *What does Catherine find when she enters Henry's room at Northanger Abbey?* A 'litter of books, guns, and great coats'. The rector of Woodston is not, we deduce, an excessively pious clergyman and enjoys country sports, like any other offspring of the landed gentry. Mr Collins, by contrast, prefers gardening.

3/20 *Why does the General not go to bed at the same time as the young ladies?* He has 'many pamphlets to finish', and will burn the midnight oil 'poring over the affairs of the nation'. If not actively engaged in military duty, is he perhaps in parliament, or a magistrate, or occupied in business for the War Office?—there is no clear indication, although he is, on one occasion that we know of, summoned to London. And Henry tells Catherine that Eleanor is often lonely at the Abbey, because her father is frequently away.

3/21 *Why does Catherine not, as she plans, steal out at midnight to investigate the 'mysterious apartments' in which, she is convinced, the General's poor wife is secretly incarcerated?* She falls asleep.

3/22 *How long was General Tilney's wife sick, before she died? And was all her family round her?* It was five days before the bilious fever carried her off. Only Eleanor was not present at her deathbed.

3/23 *It is a week between James's letter from Oxford, announcing that it is all over with his engagement, and Isabella's letter from Bath (which the family are hurriedly leaving) intimating that it is all over between herself and Captain Tilney (who has, treacherously, transferred his affections to Charlotte Davis). What has happened in this interval?* Something disgraceful. Probably not seduction (Isabella is too wily for that) but probably a major indiscretion. It may be that Frederick was deliberately sabotaging the threatened Morland–Thorpe union on Henry's behalf, with Henry's connivance. More likely, however, is that Captain Tilney grew bored with Isabella (as who would not?) and ostentatiously transferred his attentions to Charlotte Davis to signal that marriage with her (Isabella) was out of the question.

3/24 *Why is Henry not at Northanger Abbey when Catherine is summarily banished?* It is Sunday and he is taking the service at Woodston.

3/25 *How much does Catherine bring to the marriage?* Three thousand pounds.

Level Four

4/1 *Who, educationally, are Catherine's teachers and what do they teach her?* Mrs Morland, we learn, teaches her infant children 'their letters' (how to read). The mornings are given over to teaching and it exhausts 'my poor mother', Catherine observes. Mrs Morland also teaches her elder girls French conversation. This is somewhat unusual, given the fact that—with England at war with France—proficiency in that language can be of little use to young ladies in Wiltshire (or Bath). On the other hand, there was nothing entirely unusual in little English girls being taught some elementary French: Jane Austen herself knew enough to read it, though apparently she could never speak it fluently. It must also be Mrs Morland who gives her girls basic instruction in such 'accomplishments' as drawing and recitation. A teacher is brought in to teach the spinet (in all of these accomplishments Catherine is reported to have been a wretched, and with the spinet a rebellious, pupil). Catherine's father teaches her to write and enough simple arithmetic to keep household accounts. It is in his library, presumably, that (around 16 years old) she starts reading Shakespeare, Pope, Gray, and Thomson. Unlike Jane Austen, Catherine never attends boarding school (even to be 'finished'). Unlike Emma Woodhouse, she has no governess. It is this unworldliness which accounts for her subsequent ingenuousness at Bath and Northanger. It does not, evidently, lessen her attractions to Henry Tilney, who clearly wants a wife unpractised in worldly ways and wiles.

4/2 *It would forestall a lot of complication (and rob us of an entertaining novel) if Henry had made enquiries of Catherine's background, her family's financial circumstances, and her relationship to the Allens. Why does he omit to do this?* It is, presumably, a tribute to his good manners and breeding. No gentleman would ever make enquiries about a young lady's background, because it would be taking her name in vain, and making her the subject of common gossip. We admire him for his ignorance on this subject.

4/3 *Catherine gets her copies of Mrs Radcliffe's terrifying tales from Isabella. Where does Isabella get them from?* One of the many Bath circulating libraries, we deduce, although it is never mentioned. They are, we know, in multi-volume form, the exclusive 'library edition' of books of the day. With three grown girls to keep occupied, a library subscription would be a wise investment for Mrs Thorpe (one book, in three volumes, could keep them all occupied at once).

4/4 *What do we learn, in this novel, about the diverse reading habits of gentlemen and ladies in the 1790s?* A lot. Women, as Isabella and Catherine's excited consumption of Mrs Radcliffe's tales indicates, often read 'together' (made easier, given the multi-volume format of library novels). Men, typically, read alone (Henry promises to read *Udolpho* aloud to Eleanor—then gets so excited he takes it off to devour in solitude). Men, we deduce, read faster than women (it takes Catherine two mornings, from after 9 o'clock until 1 o'clock, to get halfway through *Udolpho*—'the veil' episode). In general, men read newspapers (or, in pompous General Tilney's case, 'pamphlets') and women fiction. In the famous 'only a novel' outburst ('and what are you reading, Miss ——?'), we are to assume it is a censorious male addressing a flibbertigibbet young lady. This gender divide is confirmed, when after taking his 'glass of water' at the Pump Room, Mr Allen, we are told, 'joined some gentlemen to talk over the politics of the day and compare the accounts of their newspapers'. Catherine humbly testifies that 'gentlemen read better books'. Men, however, clearly do indulge in fiction—if somewhat furtively. Henry knows Radcliffe well enough to parody her, hilariously (men, he later tells an amazed Catherine, read 'nearly as many [novels] as women'). John Thorpe has, we know, finished two novels. Tellingly, they are the improper *Tom Jones* and the notoriously pornographic *The Monk*, by Matthew Lewis. Neither is a book that a respectable young lady would be permitted by her guardians to read. (On the other hand, we know that Jane Austen read *Tom Jones*, as witnessed in her early letters. Her family may have been freer about such things than others.)

4/5 *How is it that Henry, a bachelor clergyman with countrified tastes, knows so much about muslin and women's dress (that is, the difference between five- and nine-shilling muslin, and that Catherine's sprigged muslin will not wash well, and will fray)?* Henry, 25 and an eligible bachelor, has been Eleanor's only companion at home, at the Abbey. He has picked up expertise about textiles and, presumably, had some practice with her in dancing (dancing was taught to boys at public school, where he would have learned the basics). When Catherine remarks on the fact that he is a good dancer, Miss Tilney smiles ironically. Henry's own ironies on the subject of women's dress, fashionable conversation, and dancing suggest a certain chauvinism. The motherless brother and sister must, we assume, have been thrown together more than was usual with young people of their class. It appears, for example, that Mrs Hughes is only a companion/chaperone to Eleanor on the one Bath visit, and not an inmate of Northanger Abbey.

4/6 *Catherine's response on seeing James drive up with John Thorpe at Cheap Street is an uncharacteristic exclamation (and near profanity): 'Good heaven! 'tis James!' Why is she so surprised?* It is Monday, 16 February. The two young men are undergraduates at Oxford. 'Pernoctation' rules would forbid their being absent, as they are, from college for two weeks. They are, bluntly, truanting.

4/7 *Catherine first identifies Henry's sister to Isabella as the 'young lady with the white beads round her head'. What do we later learn about these beads?* Later, Mrs Allen says: 'I am sure Mrs Tilney is dead, because Mrs Hughes [Eleanor's chaperone] told me there was a very beautiful set of pearls that Mr Drummond gave his daughter on her wedding-day and that Miss Tilney has got now, for they were put by for her when her mother died.' It is a mark of Catherine's ingenuousness that she does not know what pearls ('white beads') are. Mrs Allen's artless remark also informs us

that the money in the Tilney family has come from the mother's
Drummond connections. General Tilney, we may further presume, was a successful fortune-hunter. What, one may ask paren-
thetically, was a 'set' of pearls? Presumably a headband, necklace
and matching bracelets, earrings, and brooches.

4/8 *As they drive, John Thorpe asks Catherine: 'Old Allen is as rich
as a Jew, is not he?' Later in the novel, he will make the same point
about General Tilney being 'rich as a Jew'. What should we read into
this apparent anti-Semitism?* That John Thorpe has been dealing
with money-lenders is one construction. Another is that he is
thinking of the fabulous wealth of banking dynasties such as the
Rothschilds, who were becoming commonly known at this
period.

4/9 *When, at the Thursday assembly in the Pump Room, John
Thorpe comes up to Catherine and says 'I thought you and I were to
dance together', she says: 'you never asked me'. She knows, and so do
we, that this is not true ('when he spoke to her [she] pretended not to
hear him'). John (with some justice) calls it 'a cursed shabby trick'. Is
it?* Catherine, we assume, is not lying but hinting, politely, that
John should desist from his attentions. He was too rude to ask
clearly and properly, assuming as he does that he is irresistible
and so there can be no question but that she will want to dance
with him, following some mumbled invitation. She is, quite
legitimately, putting him in his place. The exchange suggests,
however, that we should not always take her ingenuousness at face
value. Later in the narrative we shall again catch her in what
might seem like a white lie.

4/10 *General Tilney, on his first inspection of Catherine, is described
as 'a very handsome man, of a commanding aspect, past the bloom,
but not past the vigour of life'. What do we know of his military
career?* Nothing, other than his rank. It is wartime, he is not
disabled by age or physical handicap; why is he not serving his
country? He may have sold his commission (money is very
important to him), retaining a courtesy rank. It may be that he is

waiting for orders from the War Office. From his taste for fruit (particularly 'pines', or pineapples) we may perhaps assume that military service took him to the West Indies, or India. He has, as far as we can make out, few military companions (the only one mentioned is General Courteney). The only companion of his whom we meet in the narrative is the wholly disreputable pup, John Thorpe, with whom he plays billiards (and certainly wins). Mysterious. Catherine's dark suspicions are not *entirely* unjustified.

4/11 *Does Catherine really not understand that John Thorpe is proposing marriage when he comes on her alone in Edgar's Buildings, before leaving for London?* Isabella, the cunning minx, would certainly understand. Catherine, we assume, is far too naive and innocent to understand John's clumsy overtures.

4/12 *Why does Henry seemingly acquiesce in his brother's campaign to seduce Isabella? What is he saying in the 'whispered conversation' that Catherine observes the brothers having, before Frederick embarks on his seduction of Isabella?* It would be nice to think that Henry is giving his wayward brother wise fraternal advice. More likely, however, Frederick is manœuvring to be introduced to Isabella. Later on, one may suspect, Henry may encourage his brother with the aim of ensuring that the odious Isabella will never be his sister-in-law. Immediately after the whispered conversation, Henry takes Catherine off, leaving the coast clear for his brother.

4/13 *Catherine utters what looks like her second untruth when she tells Isabella that 'I did not see [John Thorpe] once that whole morning' when—as the reader will recall—the young man came to her alone, in Edgar's Buildings, to declare love and propose marriage (not something a young girl would readily forget). Catherine backtracks slightly by saying later, 'for the life of me, I cannot recollect it.' How should one react to this lapse of memory?* Were Catherine Isabella, we might suspect duplicity (lying in the cause of true love is no sin). Given what we know of her innocence about the world, it is clear that she never understood that John was, in his way, proposing; hence his conversation with her went straight out of her mind.

4/14 *'What can your brother mean?', Catherine enquires of Henry, when his brother ostentatiously pays court to Isabella. What does Frederick mean?* It is a good question. It could be seduction (he wants to 'ruin' her) or, more likely, flirtation (he merely wants a few days' distraction, before going off—perhaps to death or glory—against the French). Or is he callously torpedoing the engagement between James and Isabella to protect his brother's (and ultimately the family's) interests? This last hypothesis is supported by Henry's surely disingenuous consolation to Catherine that Frederick's 'leave of absence will soon expire, and he must return to his regiment—And what will then be their acquaintance?—The mess-room will drink Isabella Thorpe for a fortnight, and she will laugh with your brother over poor Tilney's passion for a month.' Henry must know the likelihood is more sinister than this. What is his game? There may, however, be a simpler and more convincing explanation: Henry can't enlighten the innocent Catherine about Frederick's callous pursuit of Isabella because she (Catherine) *is* innocent, and because she is James's sister.

4/15 *What is the implication of Frederick's graceless farewell: 'How glad I shall be when you are all off'?* An empty apartment is always useful to a young officer on the loose. And, of course, he may merely be fed up with Papa scolding him as if he were still a schoolboy.

4/16 *Why, female light-headedness apart, is Catherine so entranced with 'castles'?* Mrs Radcliffe's *Udolpho* is clearly a culprit. But, less to the young lady's discredit, old echoing castles appeal to her because they are large and empty. The parsonage at Fullerton contains as many as ten children, two adults, and a cohort of servants. In his teasing, it is the huge, sinister, vacancy of the Abbey that Henry plays on. The long, dusky corridors, the huge, vaulted halls, the many dusty apartments. And no one (least of all nine siblings) to be seen. On her first meal at General Tilney's table, Catherine is most of all struck by the 'spaciousness' of the dining hall.

4/17 *Why does Jane Austen specifically tell us that Catherine has a 'charming game of play with a litter of puppies just able to roll about' in Henry's stable-yard at Woodston?* Because this shows that she is an instinctively affectionate country-bred girl, without any squeamish fears of getting her hands or dress dirty (we cannot imagine the flashily smart suburban flirt Isabella demeaning herself to romp with puppies), and so will be a good kind mother to future messy little babies of her own. Henry and Eleanor have already observed Catherine's character and Eleanor makes it clear that she would be very happy if her brother did marry Catherine. He, however, needs to have this visual proof of her kind-heartedness.

4/18 *Why has the General put his sons into 'professions'? 'Employment', he says, is a good thing, even if one has private means. Why then does he have no employment, as far as we can make out?* The General is careful to qualify his generalization by adding that it is good for *young* people. Not always a fool or a villain, he has evidently seen how easy it is for a rich young man to squander the family fortune if he has no occupation to engage his interest. Henry will be disposed of to the family living. The General is probably (thanks to the war) glad to have Frederick away from home and not under his feet (or, worse, dissipating himself in London or some watering place).

4/19 *In the company of Henry and Eleanor, General Tilney clearly seems to think that Catherine is the Allens' heiress (basing this on John Thorpe's misinformation). Are Eleanor and Henry similarly deceived as to Catherine's wealth and handsome prospects?* Surely not. Eleanor will have noted Catherine's modest wardrobe and lack of valuable jewels. Henry, who is sharp enough, may— despite his good manners—have made some enquiry and have satisfied himself that, although not penniless, Catherine is not a great prize in money terms. As we learn later, he has his own financial independence from his mother's marriage settlement. He is not dependent on his father. He may even want his father, snob and fortune-hunter that he is, to be discomfited.

4/20 *Why has Eleanor not yet married?* She has an unnamed admirer who only becomes acceptable to the General as his son-in-law when he unexpectedly inherits a viscountcy. It may be, too, that the General, in his selfishness, is not displeased to keep her at home. Eleanor, unmarried, saves him the expense of a dowry. Who, one wonders, will serve as hostess at the Abbey when Eleanor leaves? Or, perhaps, like the married George and Emma Knightley, the newly-weds will take up residence at the Abbey.

4/21 *In his famous denunciation of Catherine's Gothic speculations, Henry talks of an England 'where every man is surrounded by a neighbourhood of voluntary spies, and where roads and newspapers lay every thing open'. What, historically, is he thinking of?* There was a lot of official espionage among the population during the French wars (Wordsworth, it is suggested, may even have spied on Coleridge). But Henry is probably thinking of the omnipresent servants and neighbours—unofficial espionage. A reading of the letters and literary remains of the Austen family at the period suggests that walls had ears. Not only that, gossip circulated at high speed.

4/22 *Why, given her preposterous and highly offensive conjectures, does Henry continue to 'indulge' Catherine, showing her, as we are told, 'rather more attention than usual'?* He has always wanted a 'simple' wife; not one of your Bath women of the world. Her gaffes certify her as, in his eyes, the genuine thing: an innocent girl. He is also very kind-hearted and willing to sympathize with Catherine for her (much regretted) foolishness.

4/23 *Catherine thinks Isabella is now engaged to Captain Tilney and that the Captain will gallop back to his father (as James rushed back to Fullerton) for paternal permission. Henry's guess is that his* *brother's marrying Isabella is 'not probable'. Has he known this from the first?* Yes.

4/24 *Catherine, on receiving the letter from Isabella describing Captain Tilney's desertion, poses a pertinent question: 'I do not understand what Captain Tilney has been about all this time. Why should he pay her such attentions as to make her quarrel with my brother, and then fly off himself?'* Why? See above. Henry, rather lamely, suggests that 'mischief' was his motive. He still cannot bring himself to tell the innocent Catherine what his brother's motives were.

4/25 *Does Eleanor really not know why her father is so 'discomposed' and so furious with Catherine?* She must have some idea. She may even have known, before the General, the true nature of Catherine's prospects (they are, by now, intimate friends).

Mansfield Park

Level One

1/1 *How many children do the Price family have, and what are their names and ages at the start of the novel's main narrative?* Mrs Price (poor woman) has ten successful pregnancies in all, and Mary dies, leaving nine surviving Price children. They are, in descending order: William, Fanny, John (offstage), Richard (offstage), Susan, Mary (deceased), Sam, Tom, Charles, and finally little Betsey. When the sisters, as recorded in the opening pages, renew contact, Mrs Price has eight children (Mary still being alive) and is expecting her ninth, Charles. Fanny, going then to Mansfield Park and never revisiting her home, does not meet Charles and Betsey until she returns to Portsmouth years later.

1/2 *How recently has Mrs Norris seen her sister, Mrs Price, at the time of the novel's main action?* She says 'she had not seen her poor dear sister Price for more than twenty years'. Even after the reconciliation which was sealed with the dispatch of Fanny, and despite the fact that she is Betsey's godmother, she has not made the relatively short (thirty-six-hour by coach) trip to Portsmouth. Presumably, (wealthy) skinflint that she is, Mrs Norris begrudges the expense of travel and overnight accommodation at an inn. Nor has Mrs Price ever been received at Mansfield Park. Which raises the question: after Fanny marries Edmund, will she be invited?

1/3 *What argument does Mrs Norris adduce for the safety of introducing a girl into the Bertram family—specifically with regard to the two young sons of the family?* 'Breed her up with them ... and suppose her even to have the beauty of an angel, and she will never be more to either than a sister.' Mary Crawford, much later, observes that Fanny does indeed have a look of Edmund sometimes—a brother–sister similarity of feature.

1/4 *Where does Miss Lee teach her three charges (Maria, Julia, and—latterly—Fanny) and what happens to the school-room?* It is the East room: so chosen because it will get the early morning light—when lessons begin. Facing east, it will also be cold, which is why Mrs Norris's prohibition on a fire being lit there, after Fanny takes it over as her study on Miss Lee's departure, is so cruel.

1/5 *Who does Mrs Norris declare can help Fanny dress herself?* Either of the housemaids (that is, not a personal attendant, but a skivvy whose normal work is room cleaning).

1/6 *How much older are Julia and Maria than Fanny?* Two and three years, respectively. Tom (a Cambridge man—who evidently spent more time at the racecourse at Newmarket than in his classroom) is seven years older, and Edmund (whose absence at Eton and Oxford is only summarily described) is a couple of years younger than Tom.

1/7 *How often does Fanny see William in the nine years she spends at Mansfield Park, and how often other members of her family?* She sees William twice. On the second occasion, when she is 18, they return together to Portsmouth. She has seen no member of her family—even on the occasion of the death of a favourite sister, Mary—in the intervening years.

1/8 *How much income does Mrs Norris have?* Six hundred pounds a year, and free tenancy in the estate's 'White House'. She is rich. Presumably her elderly husband was as frugal as she.

1/9 *What advantageous physical attributes does Henry Crawford possess?* He has good teeth, a pleasing address, 'so much countenance', and is 'well made' (that is, he has an athletic figure). But he is said to be 'plain' and, as the lofty (but stupid) Mr Rushworth points out, is short in stature—ambiguously five foot eight or nine inches. From which we may assume that Rushworth is a bulky six-footer.

1/10 *What does Dr Grant think to be 'an insipid fruit at the best'?* Apricots, thus condemning Mrs Norris's boasts about her superior Moor Park tree.

1/11 *Why has Mary Crawford never ridden a horse, before coming to Mansfield (and appropriating Fanny's steed)?* It is odd. One assumes that her life has been entirely metropolitan and that she has never even spent any time at Everingham. But riding is not a universal attainment among the women in Jane Austen's world (can Emma ride, or Elizabeth?).

1/12 *Who sits alongside Henry on the 'barouche box' on the visit to Sotherton?* 'Happy Julia'. Maria seethes. It is, of course, Mrs Grant who has placed Julia there as the eligible sister, hoping, evidently, that a match might be made. Maria is spoken for.

1/13 *What are the 'curious pheasants'?* Ornamental breeds, as opposed to the preserved birds which Mr Rushworth's keepers raise at Sotherton. The ornamental birds were for ladies, as decorative garden pets. The preserved pheasants, in the nearby woods and moors, were for gentlemen to shoot.

1/14 *Why did Mrs Whitaker, the housekeeper at Sotherton, turn away two housemaids?* For wearing white gowns—a privilege reserved for the ladies of the house. Fanny, for example, has a white gown at her first dinner party; as Edmund gallantly says on that occasion, 'A woman can never be too fine while she is all in white.' A woman, but not a maidservant.

1/15 *What is Fanny Price's favourite reading?* Poetry, biography, and improving essays. Not, definitely not, fiction.

1/16 *Who is driven from home by a green goose?* Henry and Mary. Their reverend brother-in-law takes offence (becomes violent, indeed) when served a bird which has not been hung long enough. Without refrigerators it is a complex thing to have a bird 'mature' enough for the table—particularly the table of the epicurean Revd Dr Grant. At least, being fifteen years older than his wife, and a glutton, he will dig his grave with his teeth in a few years.

1/17 *Where did Tom Bertram meet the Honourable John Yates?* At Weymouth, playground of wastrels in Austen's fiction.

1/18 *Who divulges to Sir Thomas that private theatricals were in prospect?* Lady Bertram, who has lazily not followed the rehearsals and knows scarcely more about it than her amazed husband.

1/19 *Who says, pathetically, 'Every body gets made but me'?* William. Promoted in the naval service, he means. He is, thanks to Admiral Crawford, eventually 'made' a lieutenant, and his career takes off.

1/20 *What does William bring Fanny from Sicily?* A 'very pretty amber cross'. Mary, symbolically, gives her a 'chain' to go with it. As she does so, Mary has a look around her eyes that Fanny 'could not be satisfied with'. As the reader will understand, Miss Crawford is scheming to capture the young girl for her brother.

1/21 *What vessel is William posted to, after his promotion to lieutenant?* 'H.M. sloop *Thrush*'.

1/22 *Who thinks the alphabet 'her greatest enemy'?* Little Betsey.

1/23 *When she says 'what a difference a vowel makes', what vowel is Mary Crawford thinking of?* The Hon. Mr John Yates 'rants' in his performance as Baron Wildenhaim. But he has not the 'rents', or income, to claim Julia as his bride.

1/24 *How much does Sir Thomas give Fanny on her departure for Portsmouth?* Ten pounds. She does not, as she might, give the money to her mother. Part of it she expends on a silver knife for Betsey, another part on membership of the Portsmouth circulating library.

1/25 *Where does Tom have the accident which precipitates the fever which leads, eventually, to his moral regeneration?* At Newmarket, drunkenly we presume, after a day at the races.

Level Two

2/1 *We are told that Lieutenant Price's profession is such as 'no interest' (specifically Sir Thomas Bertram's) could reach. Is this true?* The Marines (a relatively newly created arm of the military services, used to keep discipline in the Royal Navy) had a very low status at this period. He might have been willing to help, but there was no powerful person with whom Sir Thomas could use his influence. Nor, for perhaps the same reason, does he help William later—although Henry, through Admiral Crawford, does.

2/2 *Why is Mrs Norris, the incarnation of selfishness, so keen that Fanny Price be brought to Mansfield Park?* It is on the face of it odd. One assumes that Mrs Norris cannot resist interfering with everyone around her and, having effectively taken over the management of Mansfield Park, she now wants to widen her circle of influence and start patronizing her youngest sister. Once Fanny arrives, Mrs Norris makes full use of her as a hard-worked personal assistant—saving herself a wage in the process.

2/3 *What can we read into the fact that Mrs Price has nine children (and more pregnancies), Lady Bertram has four children, and Mrs Norris none?* Mrs Price is the victim of her husband's undisciplined appetites—released only by menopause. Sir Thomas is, by contrast, 'restrained'. Mrs Norris, perhaps because of her husband's age and gout, perhaps because of his 'narrow income' and her parsimony, has restrained herself absolutely.

2/4 *What is Fanny's principal physical attraction?* Henry Crawford admires 'that soft skin of her's, so frequently tinged with a blush', and Mary Crawford agrees that 'she has a sweet smile'. She is the only character said to 'blush' in the novel.

Her complexion is, in fact, a kind of litmus paper. She wilts in Portsmouth, 'colours' when morally affronted, and goes pale when, for any period, plunged into unhappiness. The diagnosis is that she needs air and exercise—hence the 'old grey poney' and regular excursions.

2/5 *Why does Lady Bertram give up the family house in town?* 'In consequence of a little ill-health, and a great deal of indolence'. There is, throughout the novel, a suggestion that she is agoraphobic—hating to leave the confinement of her drawing-room. It is odd, too, that Sir Thomas, being in Parliament, does not insist on keeping it.

2/6 *Sir Thomas's comment that William, when he comes to Mansfield Park, 'must find his sister at sixteen in some respects too much like his sister at ten' induces bitter tears in Fanny. What does the remark mean?* That she is still shy and schoolgirlish at the age of 16. It is unfair since, for seven years, her upbringing has been in his hands. Maria and Julia are, by contrast, naturally self-confident young ladies. In their presence, Mary Crawford finds it difficult to believe that Fanny is 'out' (that is, marriageable).

2/7 *What are the Crawfords worth, and why do they come to stay with the Grants at Mansfield Park?* Henry has a good estate in Norfolk worth £4,000 a year, Mary a fortune of £20,000. Her fortune makes it somewhat surprising that she should contemplate, however flightily, marriage with Edmund—particularly after she discovers he intends to be a country parson (see her contemptuous remark, 'I had not imagined a country parson ever aspired to a shrubbery'). Mary cannot stay in the Hill Street house of her uncle, the 'vicious' Admiral Crawford after he brings his mistress to live with him, his wife having died (the Admiral's wife, we are told, doted on Mary; she was evidently cooler towards her nephew). Henry is oddly averse to Norfolk—he is, indeed, averse to any 'permanence of abode or limitation of society'. He lacks, of course, any occupation beyond that of 'improving' his own, and his friends', estates.

2/8 *How many kinds of horse-drawn vehicle are mentioned in the narrative?* The cart that was at one point intended to bring Mary Crawford's harp to Mansfield; Henry Crawford's barouche (which does, in the event, bring the harp); the Bertram family carriage (whose 'steady old coachman' also serves as young Fanny's groom, when she rides; later, the carriage takes Fanny to her first dinner party at the Parsonage); Lady Bertram's post-chaise; Mr Rushworth's curricle (he also has a chaise); old Mrs Rushworth's chariot; the hired post-chaise which takes William and Fanny to Portsmouth.

2/9 *Why is Mary so long in discovering (not until they find themselves in the chapel at Sotherton) that Edmund is destined for the Church?* She evidently does not have a close relationship with her half-sister, Mrs Grant, who would certainly know (since Dr Grant has popped in between Edmund and his destined living at Mansfield). It also witnesses to a certain levity in Mary that she should assume—as she evidently does—that a young man like Edmund would (like Henry) do nothing in life, but live on unearned income. And, for the young men she is thinking of, 'a clergyman is nothing'.

2/10 *Which couple takes a 'serpentine course' in the novel, and what are the implications of the phrase?* Edmund and Mary, in the wood at Sotherton, with Fanny modestly in attendance. Mary, of course, is playing the Edenic temptress, urging him to stray from the path of clerical duty. Which, were she to give him more encouragement, he might well (despite the good influence of Fanny) do.

2/11 *Why do we not admire Maria Bertram for squeezing through the spiked fence at Sotherton (something that Fanny, even if she were wanton enough to do it, has not the strength to accomplish)? How should we picture this fence?* The breaking of bounds is something that only men may do. The physical obstacle is, presumably, as follows. A ha-ha (which by definition is a revetted ditch *without* any fence on the top) divides the Sotherton gardens from the park beyond. But to get into the park, you have to cross this ditch—so presumably a stretch some six feet wide is left undug for a pathway. But then animals could come up the pathway, so you have to have gates at the garden end—tall gates, so that no beast can take a straightforward running jump and get over. This still leaves the possibility that some clever beast could clamber or jump diagonally from the path past the gatepost, and enter the garden that way. So the next step is to provide some lower railing—*cheval de frise*—on each side of the iron gateposts. There are smaller spikes

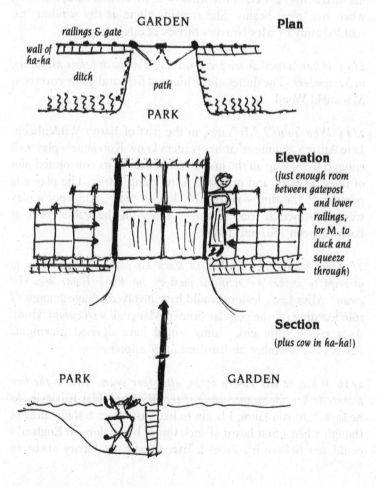

Plan

GARDEN

railings & gate

wall of
ha-ha

ditch

path

PARK

Elevation

(just enough room
between gatepost
and lower
railings,
for M. to
duck and
squeeze
through)

Section

(plus cow in ha-ha!)

PARK   GARDEN

each side, tall iron gates in the centre. Henry, Maria, and Julia manage to squeeze through between the gatepost and the lower range of spikes, and still find foothold on the path the other side. In all probability they squeeze through rather than clamber over—to swing their legs across would be really rather improper for the Miss Bertrams.

2/12 *Who gives whom a lesson on astronomy, and with what results?* Edmund instructs Fanny in 'star-gazing'. He breaks off his instruction to her, at the window at Mansfield Park, however, when the 'glee' begins. She remains alone at the window 'till scolded away by Mrs Norris's threats of catching cold'.

2/13 *What 'duties' do we presume bring Tom back before his father, in September?* The duties of the hunting field and game coverts in Mansfield Wood.

2/14 *Who 'rants'?* Mr Yates, in the part of Baron Wildenhaim. Jane Austen assumes that her readers know Kotzebue's play well enough to pick up all the in-joke references to its convoluted plot of illicit amours, and marriage plans going astray. The play was popular at the time—regrettably less so today. Kotzebue's play was performed at least seventeen times on the public stage at Bath between 1801 and 1806.

2/15 *In helping Mr Rushworth learn his part, Fanny is said to attempt to make 'an artificial memory for him'. What does this mean?* Miss Lee's lessons would have involved a huge amount of rote learning (of the popular primer, Mangnall's *Questions*, kind). As a clever little girl, Fanny would have devised mnemonic devices to remember his 'two and forty' speeches

2/16 *When he sees Fanny again, after four years, what is the first feature in her appearance which strikes William?* Her hairstyle. As he says, 'Do you know, I begin to like that queer fashion already, though when I first heard of such things being done in England I could not believe it'. From a later remark by Henry about an errant curl falling down on to Fanny's brow, we assume that the style, at this point in time, is for an upswept coiffure.

2/17 *Why cannot Fanny play an instrument—the piano (like her cousins) or the harp (like Mary)?* Fanny said, on arrival at Mansfield Park, that she did not want to learn music. Doubtless she was terrified by the prospect of mockery from Julia and Maria, already playing duets. She has consoled herself with reading and 'poetry' (from Sir Thomas's library) and is the better, and more cultivated, for it.

2/18 *Why is Mrs Norris so obsessed with saving Sir Thomas money (in such matters as forbidding any fire in Fanny's East room)?* She has appointed herself, we guess, the mistress of the house at Mansfield Park. Doubtless she contrives to skim some useful profit to herself from the housekeeping and weekly accounts. Lady Bertram, of course, is far too indolent to attend to such things, and someone must.

2/19 *What Shakespeare play does Fanny read to Lady Bertram, and what is its significance?* It is *Henry VIII*. Divorce is hinted at, later in the narrative.

2/20 *Why does Fanny insist (justifying her rejection of Henry) that 'we have not one taste in common', when they have recently been concurring in their love of Shakespeare, both of them knowledgeably?* She is rationalizing her instinctive feelings about his character. In fact, in terms of intelligence and native wit, she and Henry would be very suitable mates.

2/21 *At what time of year is Fanny packed off to Portsmouth?* 'The dirty month of February'. Given the fact that she is chronically 'delicate' (and given the prevalence of contagious diseases such as consumption in cramped urban houses), Sir Thomas is forgetting the possible risk to her health and well-being. He none the less conceives what he is doing as 'medicinal' (morally, that is).

2/22 *What is the principal cause of quarrel between Susan and Betsey, and what is its cure?* A silver knife, bequeathed by the deceased little sister, Mary. It is, evidently, the only family silver the Price family possesses. Fanny resolves the conflict by buying another silver knife, for Betsey.

2/23 *Why is Henry 'not satisfied about Maddison'?* Maddison is, one gathers, Henry's agent in his estate at Everingham which, until Fanny shows him the error of his ways, Henry has neglected. He fears that Maddison 'means to impose on me, if possible, and get a cousin of his own into a certain mill, which I design for somebody else'. It is very likely that Henry is, with this Maddison business, primarily concerned to ingratiate himself with Fanny by bringing to her attention his new sensitivity to the responsibilities of being master of Everingham.

2/24 *How would Fanny's father, as he protests, deal with the delinquent Maria Rushworth?* 'I'd give her the rope's end as long as I could stand over her.'

2/25 *What is Lady Bertram's exclamation, when Fanny returns to a devastated Mansfield?* 'Dear Fanny! now I shall be comfortable.' First things first.

Level Three

3/1 *What, with regard to family planning, should we read into the first words of the novel, 'About thirty years ago'?* Given the fact that the eldest of the Bertram children, Tom, is 25, it would seem that Sir Thomas and Lady Bertram practised admirable restraint as to family planning. Mrs Price, with her nine living children and one (that we know of) dead, evidently practised less.

3/2 *When the juvenile Edmund sends his cousin William half a guinea 'under the seal' what does this indicate?* The money, for safety, is put under the hot wax which seals the folded sheets of the letter (envelopes, as we know them, were not invented until later in the nineteenth century). But the seal will also display the arms of the Bertram family, establishing it as an (for the hopeful recipient) act of patronage.

3/3 *Why does Edmund not get the family living of Mansfield when his uncle Norris dies?* Because of Tom's extravagance, which has run the family into debt. The death of the Revd Mr Norris occurs when Fanny is 'about fifteen' which means that Tom must be about 21. Presumably his debts (from his later presence at Newmarket) are the consequence of gambling and what the novel calls 'bad connections'. As the heir, his delinquencies are dealt with indulgently. Sir Thomas has been obliged to sell a life interest in the living to the Revd Dr Grant, for cash, rather than installing a *locum tenens* curate for the four or five years prior to Edmund's ordination.

3/4 *Why does the lively, young, beautiful, and intelligent Maria Bertram accept the stupid Mr Rushworth (that is, not worth a light, or 'rush light')?* Because 'marriage with Mr Rushworth would give her the enjoyment of a larger income than her father's, as well as ensure her the house in town, which was now a prime object'. Sir Thomas, as a number of comments indicate, has kept his daughters confined in the Park (Fanny likewise, is prohibited from even a visit to her family—her 'home' as she thinks it—at Portsmouth; and from comments later in the novel, it is clear that she has never, in her eighteen years, been to London). When the newly married Mrs Rushworth goes to Brighton we are told that 'Every public place was new to Maria'—and sexually exciting, associated as it is with the Prince Regent. Sir Thomas's caution about his daughters, and his niece, is destined to backfire.

3/5 *Why has Tom, as we are told, given Fanny a profusion of work-boxes and netting-boxes?* One assumes they are successive birthday presents. Every genteel lady needed to have some appropriate handicraft to keep herself occupied in the drawing-room, after dinner. This was nearly always sewing: married women would

make endless baby clothes, young maidens would work at hand-
kerchiefs, neckerchiefs, collars, and so on. There was, rather confusingly, both 'netting' and 'knitting' (the humbler occupation,
associated with the domestic work of lower- or lower-middle-
class females).

3/6 *Who profits most from the aborted production of* Lovers' Vows
at Mansfield Park? Mrs Norris, who makes off with the roll of
green baize, destined to be the theatre curtains. The fabric 'went
off with her to her cottage, where she happened to be particularly
in want of green baize'. Green baize and drugget were valued as
covering for carpets, to prevent wear and tear (a precaution which
would have been dear to Mrs Norris's heart).

3/7 *What is Fanny's 'favourite indulgence'?* 'Being suffered to sit
silent and unattended to'. This is described during her first 'solo'
visit to the Parsonage, but earlier we were told how, when her
aunts had exhausted her, with rose-cutting and walking in the
heat, she retreated, in her prostration, to a distant sofa from
which an indignant Edmund roused her.

3/8 *What is the sole occasion in the novel in which we are told that
Fanny (almost) feels hatred for another human being?* When Henry
Crawford, having interfered so callously with the affections of the
Misses Bertram, says, in Fanny's hearing, 'So! Rushworth and his
fair bride are at Brighton, I understand—Happy man!' It is this
remark, seared into her consciousness, which evidently convinces
Fanny (later) that she could never marry the man who made it—
however many cottagers he takes new interest in at Everingham.

3/9 *How much is Edmund's promised living at Thornton Lacey
worth to him?* 'Not less than seven hundred a year'. The other
living, possessed currently by Dr Grant, is worth nearly £1,000.
But the original intention was that Edmund should have the
benefit of both, and have one looked after by an impecunious
curate.

3/10 *When Edmund tells Fanny that she and Mary are 'the two dearest objects I have on earth' is he aware that he is both raising and dashing her hopes?* At some level, he must know that Fanny adores him and will seize on such compliments. Her hopes can only be controlled by what the narrative calls her 'heroism of principle'. There is always the lurking suspicion that Edmund, obtuse in his analysis of those around him, is not worthy of his cousin.

3/11 *What does Fanny have round her neck at her first ball?* Something to please everyone. Mary Crawford's (in fact Henry's) necklace and William's amber cross, the latter held at her throat by the chain which Edmund has given her. Thus arrayed, to her amazement, she leads the ball ('The distinction was too great,' she thinks. 'It was treating her like her cousins!').

3/12 *When, towards the end of Fanny's first ball, William comes up to her 'for a moment to visit her and working away his partner's fan as if for life', what does this mean?* He is giving his wilting partner refreshing air, using her fan for the purpose.

3/13 *How many card-games are depicted as being played in the narrative, and what do they imply?* Whist is played for small stakes (shillings and half-guineas); it is evidently a favourite of the older generation—notably the avaricious Mrs Norris. The principals play a game of Speculation (a kind of poker), in which their own futures and destinies are hinted at. Lady Bertram likes to play cribbage, or 'crib', with the obedient Fanny in the evenings. The young woman is, indeed, cribbed and confined.

3/14 *Why is Sir Thomas a self-confessed 'advocate for early marriages'?* He is thinking, primarily, of his heir Tom whom he wishes to settle down. And, of course, it removes young women from harm's way. We know nothing of Sir Thomas's own family background. He evidently came into his inheritance early, unencumbered by long-living parents or siblings—and married early.

3/15 *When Henry Crawford makes his proposal to Fanny, he first requests permission of Sir Thomas to do so—she being only 18, and three years beneath the age of marrying without parental consent. Why does not Henry apply to Fanny's father, at Portsmouth?* Fanny seems, de facto, to have been adopted. The legal position is, however, that Lieutenant Price (if he were mad enough to do so) could object.

3/16 *Why does Fanny (in near destitution at Portsmouth) exclaim to herself about Edmund and Mary, 'He will marry her, and be poor and miserable', when Mary has a £20,000 fortune, Edmund has a living worth over £700 a year, and they both have extremely rich, and favourably inclined, relatives?* Fanny, we must deduce, is irrational with jealousy and apprehension. Or, perhaps, she fears that even this wealth will not last long in smart London life.

3/17 *Fanny, when given intelligence about her cousins' activities in London, is disposed to think that the city is 'very much at war with all respectable attachments'. Has she ever visited the capital?* Not that we know. Sir Thomas (and his agoraphobic wife) keep their young women very close, fenced in at Mansfield Park.

3/18 *How penurious are the Price family, in their Portsmouth habitation?* They have recently moved house and, from Mrs Price's constant complaints about carpets and the slatternly maidservant Rebecca, assisted by the equally slatternly Sally (a board girl, presumably), they have clearly come down in the world. Lieutenant Price cannot afford his own newspaper (although he has money for strong spirits). There is only one candle in the house, in winter, to read the paper by (plunged into domestic gloom, Fanny is unable to read her books). He is, presumably, as a disabled officer, on half pay. Mrs Price's constant complaints about servant difficulties hark back to the more comfortable conditions of her childhood and, possibly, her early marriage when— as a young rather than a superannuated officer—her lieutenant husband's prospects (and credit) were strong. Sir Thomas has assisted Mrs Price liberally in the education and careers of her sons—this might explain the resentment which her father evidently feels against 'Fan', as he irritatingly calls her.

3/19 *What godparents are identified in the narrative?* 'Old Mrs Admiral Maxwell' is, we are told, the godparent of the deceased child Mary. This death (and possibly the death of the Admiral) may account for Lieutenant Price's failure to gain promotion in twenty years. Mrs Norris is the godmother of Betsey (an act following the reconciliation of the sisters), which perhaps indicates that Mrs Norris's Christian name is Elizabeth. But she has never seen the child, nor sent her any gift. Mrs Norris was evidently invited to stand as godmother, with the hope that she would eventually do for Betsey what had been done for Fanny. Sir Thomas and Lady Bertram are sponsors for the ninth baby, Charles Price. They too, it seems, have never seen the child (8 years old at the time of the main narrative).

3/20 *Why is Fanny so surprised when her father behaves in a gentlemanlike way on meeting Mr Crawford?* She knows so little of military life and protocol that she does not realize that he is addressing him as he might a superior officer. Fanny has never seen her father in his occupation—merely as a domestic brute, dealing with his family as he would with the lower-deck riff-raff.

3/21 *What do we deduce from the description that Sunday dresses the Price family 'in their cleanest skins and best attire'?* Saturday night, as traditional with the lower-middle classes, is bath night—although 'bath', in a household like the Prices', probably meant scrubbing over basins in strip washes. It would have been something which would have borne painfully on Fanny, after her years at Mansfield Park, with its more generous arrangements.

3/22 *What finally disillusions Edmund about Mary?* Her pragmatic analysis that, if Maria and Henry wished to be (adulterous) lovers, they should have done it with 'common discretion', not damaging publicity. It revealed to her former admirer Mary's 'blunted delicacy and . . . corrupted, vitiated, mind'. Others, less high-minded, might see it as 'sense'.

3/23 *What is the last expression which Edmund sees on Mary's face, before leaving her for ever?* 'A saucy, playful smile'. He is tempted, but 'walks on'—to Fanny whose smiles, whatever else, are never saucy.

3/24 *Where ('another country') do we deduce that Mrs Norris and the 'unfortunate Maria' are consigned to?* The word 'country' is misleading for the modern reader. To Jane Austen's contemporary readers it would have meant 'some other district in England', not foreign exile.

3/25 *What happy event crowns the conclusion of the novel?* The death of Dr Grant, and the transfer (now that he is dead) of the Mansfield living to Edmund. Together with that of Thornton Lacey, it means for the newly married Bertrams an annual income of around £1,500. The coy remark that it was at a period when the Revd and Mrs Bertram 'had begun to want an increase of income' suggests that Fanny is with child, or that they already have a small family.

Level Four

4/1 *Jane Austen gave a great deal of thought to titles (how different, for example, our sense of* Pride and Prejudice *would be were it 'First Impressions'). Why is this her sole topographical title—instead of calling it, say,* Fanny Price? Names and titles in Austen are often subtly loaded: here 'man', 'field', 'park'. What makes a field a park? Man's improvement of the land. He can, Henry tells Edmund, turn Thornton Lacey from a mere gentleman-parson's rectory (with a disfiguring farmyard, three fields and a stream adjoining) into something worthwhile. 'You may', he tells Edmund, 'give it a higher character. You may raise it into a *place*'. Henry is thinking of the current vogue for tasteful landscape 'improvement'. But moral improvement—specifically improvement of the country's leaders (such as the Bertram family) is also a theme. Fanny is entirely passive in the novel—incapable ever of speaking her thoughts and recorded as being angry only once in her life. She is, in short, little more than an 'ingredient'—a purifying, improving ingredient, into the complex mix of English upper-class society. Had Jane Austen opted for an abstract title, 'Improvement' might have served well. In terms of narrative, Mansfield Park is the place which is central to, and largely organizes, the lives of the dramatis personae. They either belong to it, or they flee it (as do the Bertram sisters), or they are exiled from it (as is Fanny). Edmund and Tom will, as sons of the household, return to it: one as the master apparent, the other as the resident clergyman.

One cannot always be certain about Jane Austen's titles. *Northanger Abbey* and *Persuasion*, for example, were probably chosen by Henry Austen posthumously. Jane refers to *Northanger Abbey* as 'Miss Catherine' when writing to her niece Fanny Knight. Henry probably called it by its published title in order to cash in on the still popular craze for Gothic thrillers. There is a family tradition that Jane referred to what we know as *Persuasion* as 'The Elliots' before her death; certainly the first French translation calls it *La Famille Elliot*.

4/2 *What do we know of the Ward family, from which the three sisters central to the ur-plot originate?* Very little. There seems to be no surviving family other than the three sisters. The only relative mentioned is the lawyer uncle, who has evidently died. The sisters, brought up in Huntingdon, were evidently possessed of great beauty and little fortune. Maria trapped the baronet, and Frances, equally beautiful, married for love a dashing lieutenant of the Marines. Elope in haste, repent in leisure. The eldest sister, having been many years on the market, had to make do with a clergyman 'with scarcely any private fortune'. From the dates in the opening sentence, it would seem that Miss Maria Ward won the heart of young Thomas Bertram (did he have his title then?) around 1780. The eventual Mrs Norris (we never know her first

name, but it may be Elizabeth—see 3/19 above) was evidently
the least attractive of the trio and obliged to make do with 'the
Rev. Mr Norris, a friend of her brother-in-law' (that is, Sir
Thomas), 'at the end of half a dozen years'—years spent
husband-hunting, we assume.

How Frances met an officer of Marines in Huntingdon is
mysterious. It evidently happened after Maria's (now Lady
Bertram's) good fortune. All Mrs Price's children are younger
than Maria's. The Marines, at this period, would have been sta-
tioned around the coast. What was Miss Frances Price doing in a
seaport like Portsmouth? Perhaps she was a governess—although
she gives no impression of intelligence or ability to educate children when we meet her in later life. Was she living with some
other branch of the Ward family? Is there (given the later
behaviour of the Bertram daughters) an 'eloping gene' in the
Ward family make-up? The marriage was, whatever the circumstances, imprudent and unlucky. Lieutenant Price (never promoted, and somehow 'disabled' in later life) never rises above that
rank. Austen (as is habitual with her) gives us little physical
description of the sisters, although the typical idleness of Lady
Bertram suggests obesity in later life and the selfish bustle of Mrs
Norris a skinnier, more athletic frame. Mrs Price we may suspect
to be worn down by her unhappy condition of life at Portsmouth.

4/3 *What should the reader make of the repeated references in the
novel to Fanny's being 'delicate and puny'?* That she would never
have survived at Portsmouth (like the tenderly remembered
Mary, she would have died in that cruel environment) and that
she is, in every way, 'fine'. Delicate has a double meaning in
reference to her: prone to illness, and superior in moral dis-
crimination. Fanny seems, as the novel progresses, to grow
stronger. But at 18 four miles' walking and picking some roses in
the sun induces total physical prostration (although, as the narrative points out, a feeling of being neglected may precipitate this
collapse). She is never, however, said to see a physician. It has
been surmised that Fanny may be anaemic—a condition not

accurately diagnosed nor treated at the time but, doubtless, common among growing girls.

4/4 *What do Sir Thomas and Tom Bertram actually do in their year or so in the Antigua estates?* Presumably they carry on an 'Organization and Method' survey, instructing the local overseer to ensure that the estate works more efficiently with what is (given the prohibition on international trade in slavery) a dwindling and ageing workforce. Young Tom would be instructed to think ahead, for the period when (without any slaves at all) he would be in charge.

4/5 *Cynically, Mary Crawford assumes that happy marriages do not exist. Which are the happiest in* Mansfield Park? That of Edmund and Fanny promises to be uniquely happy. Otherwise the torpid and emotionless union of Sir Thomas and Lady Bertram is the only barely tolerable marital relationship.

4/6 *There is current disagreement about whether Jane Austen would have picked up (or, horrible to think, have intended) the* double entendre *which strikes us so embarrassingly, in Mary Crawford's comment, 'Certainly, my home at my uncle's brought me acquainted with a circle of admirals. Of* Rears *and* Vices, *I saw enough. No, do not be suspecting me of a pun, I entreat'. Or two puns? Is this a reference to nautical homosexuality?* It is hard to believe that Jane Austen was unaware of the possible *double entendre*. But the consensus of opinion among experts (recently chewed over in the correspondence columns of the *TLS*) is that she would have been unlikely to perpetrate any such impropriety in her narrative.

4/7 *What is the objection to theatricals at Mansfield Park?* Principally that Sir Thomas's 'decorum' would be offended. But also the contaminating effect on the young ladies. Sir Thomas, as Edmund says, 'would never wish his grown up daughters to be acting plays' (children and pantomimes are obviously something else). Acting is, as Edmund says, 'a trade'—and one which is associated with loose morals.

4/8 *What part in* Lovers' Vows *is Fanny, twice, invited (commanded) to play, and would she have agreed?* She is first cast (without her consent) as the Cottager's wife—the part allocated to the luckless governess at Ecclesford. Then Mrs Grant steps in. Then Dr Grant (thanks to a tough pheasant) falls ill, and the command is renewed. 'She must yield', thinks Fanny, since Edmund asks her so persistently. Then she is saved by the return of Sir Thomas. She would, presumably, have given in.

4/9 *Why is Sir Thomas so affectionate ('Why do not I see my little Fanny?') towards his niece when he returns from Antigua?* One assumes that she, unlike his daughters, has been assiduous in writing to him, and that he has had time, during the voyage, to reflect on her moral worth (and, quite possibly, Tom's lack of that quality). And, on his return, he discovers her to be 'very pretty'—her figure and complexion 'so improved'. She has, at last, achieved the pleasing figure of a woman, we deduce.

4/10 *One of the most famous moments in the novel is that in which Fanny recalls asking her uncle 'about the slave trade last night'. The question was, as she further recalls, followed by 'a dead silence'. What, if pressed, would Sir Thomas have said?* We do not know (as with Mr Rushworth) what his political sentiments may be. But, presumably, as someone so ostentatiously earnest and decorous, he would approve of the Wilberforce Act abolishing the slave trade in 1807. And, as a large holder of plantations in the West Indies (and dependent on the income they generate) he would equally approve of the use of slave labour in those distant regions. Or, since silence is always ambiguous, it may be that he has mixed views on the subject. Another possibility is that he does not think such 'political' questions are fit to be discussed with ladies in the drawing-room: they are matter for Parliament.

4/11 *How long have the Grants been in possession of the Parsonage before Fanny is invited into the house?* Some three to four years— as a guest, that is. One assumes, however, that she has been there doing errands for, principally, Lady Bertram and Mrs Norris.

Presumably she used the servants' entrance and was not 'received'. It will be a big thing for her to attend a dinner party, and signals, as Sir Thomas intends, that she is both 'out', and in (his favour). Lady Bertram is only concerned that there be some-one to make her tea in Fanny's absence.

4/12 *When Fanny exclaims, 'there is nobleness in the name of Edmund. It is a name of heroism and renown . . . and seems to breathe the spirit of chivalry', what do we assume she has been reading?* Edmund Spenser's *Faerie Queene*. It is a nice question where she gets her books—from the Mansfield Park library presumably (she is a complete stranger to circulating libraries until her visit to Portsmouth, when she joins one with the intention of instructing her sister Susan). An old folio of Spenser would have been appropriate decor for Sir Thomas's library. We also learn, rela-tively late in the narrative, that Fanny buys books for herself—so she is assembling her own library.

4/13 *What gratification does Henry Crawford admit to have derived from the theatricals at Mansfield Park, disastrous as they were for others?* 'There was such an interest, such an animation, such a spirit diffused! Every body felt it. We were all alive.' Fanny's private comment is 'Oh! what a corrupted mind!' But Crawford's feeling is, evidently, genuine. He likes danger, likes risk, likes flirting with catastrophe not because, like the vicious Admiral his uncle, he is depraved; but because it gives him the sensation of being vital, living.

4/14 *We are told that Henry Crawford 'had once seen Fanny dance . . . but in fact he could not for the life of him recall what her dancing had been'. When was this?* He observed her at an impromptu family dance, as we are earlier told. It is significant that he has stored away this image of her. He clearly has an eye for feminine form.

4/15 *Why does Henry Crawford (if it is a private resolution) tell his sister, Mary, that 'my plan is to make Fanny Price in love with me'?*

She is not, of course, deluded that (at this stage) his intention is to marry her. He merely wants a conquest ('Is she prudish?'). Why confide this unworthy plan to another woman? Presumably he wants Mary's help in his contemptible campaign and both of them are, as Fanny inwardly suspects, corrupted morally and not above a little *Liaisons dangereuses* recreation, to while away the short days and long nights in Northamptonshire. That Mary is so complaisant makes for one of the most shocking moments in the narrative. As the narrator observes, 'she left Fanny to her fate' (a broken heart, or—given Henry's later conduct with Maria— seduction). It is striking, too, that this is one of the two or three scenes in the novel which take place beyond Fanny's range of overhearing or witnessing.

4/16 *When Edmund goes off to be ordained, and stays with the Owen family, Mary apprehends that his friend Mr Owen 'had sisters —He might find them attractive'. Why is she never jealous of Fanny?* It evidently never crosses her mind that someone as meek as Miss Price (who cannot even play an instrument) could be a rival—although her assistance in Henry's campaign to 'make Fanny Price love me' may be motivated by a covert desire to put the young lady well and truly out of play.

4/17 *Mary calls her brother's plan to make Fanny fall in love with him a 'wicked project'. How wicked? Does he intend seduction?* Yes, we may deduce. Fanny is, after all, a person of little consequence. If he treats 'ladies' as he does, we may assume that Henry has left behind him a string of ruined servant girls and other sexual victims of the lower classes. He is no respecter of propriety.

4/18 *Admiral Crawford (like Miss Lee) is a felt, but never seen presence in the novel. He is roundly described as 'vicious'. Mary suspects that Henry's manners may have been 'hurt by the contagion of his'. Does the remark have any overtones?* Contagion may, plausibly, carry an implication of the contagious disease (associated with sexual immorality) that is everywhere, but never mentioned, in the nineteenth-century novel. The Admiral's immorality lours, like a dark cloud, just over the horizon of the novel.

4/19 *As she leads the ball, Fanny thinks of her cousins, Julia and Maria, 'so often as she had heard them wish for a ball at home as the greatest of all felicities'—a felicity evidently denied these beautiful and eligible young women. Why has Sir Thomas decided to throw a ball for Fanny?* One has to assume that something profound has happened to him while in Antigua. It is said that Fanny undergoes great physical change in this period—acquiring the 'bloom' which is so important to Jane Austen's heroines. It is possible that Julia and Maria make their debut, however, while Sir Thomas and his son are away on his Antiguan business and Edmund at Oxford—so with no host at home at the Park the all-important date in their growing up passes by without ceremony. They must have come across eligible young men like Mr Rushworth at local balls (it seems that neither of them, and certainly not Fanny, has been to the great marriage mart at Bath).

4/20 *Apropos of his 'improving' tendencies, Henry Crawford lightly says, 'I never do wrong without gaining by it'. Is this the final outcome for him in the novel?* No. Had Fanny accepted him, she might, perhaps, have corrected his morals. What is interesting about the statement is the implication that Henry—whose motives are not always easy to make sense of—has a personal 'philosophy'.

4/21 *'I am quite determined to marry Fanny Price', says Henry. Why?* He is always challenged by resistance, needing—if necessary at the cost of his own, or others', destruction—to overcome it. Fanny evidently does not want to marry him. Therefore, as he conceives it, she *must*. At the melodramatic climax of the novel Henry is impelled (madness) to elope with Maria Rushworth because, initially, she receives him 'with a coldness which ought to have been repulsive . . . but he was mortified, he could not bear to be thrown off by the woman whose smiles had been so wholly at his command . . . he must get the better of it, and make

Mrs Rushworth Maria Bertram again in her treatment of him-self'. The actual elopement, however, may have been triggered by her forcing his hand (perhaps by turning up, late at night, at his door). See the comment: 'all that followed was the result of her imprudence; and he went off with her at last, *because he could not help it . . .*'

4/22 *One of Sir Thomas's strongest arguments in his first conversation, persuading Fanny to accept Henry's proposal, is that she should think of the 'advantage of your family'. 'You think only of yourself', he accuses. Is his argument strong?* Yes, there is something selfish in Fanny's moral rectitude. It should be noted, however, that in the two great crises of moral decision—whether to accept the role of Cottager's wife in *Lovers' Vows*, and whether to accept Henry's renewed proposal—she is on the brink of giving in when, fortuitously, she is saved by providential intervention (the unexpected return of Sir Thomas, the even less expected elopement of Henry with Maria).

4/23 *'As a by-stander,' Fanny tells Edmund when explaining her rejection of Henry's proposal, 'perhaps I saw more than you did'. Is this true?* Fanny is the most perspicacious character in the novel, although the least prone to speak her mind. It would, for example, be interesting to know what she really thinks of Mrs Norris—being in a better position than any one else at Mansfield Park to see the small-mindedness and meanness of the woman. When she is finally elevated by matrimony, will she be more assertive, combining depth of perception with forcefulness of expression? Or, more likely, will it require time and maturity before Fanny can see Mrs Norris (and others like her) as clearly as Jane Austen has the reader see her? There will be the added complication that, in all likelihood, Mrs Norris will only rarely come into contact with Mrs Edmund Bertram.

4/24 *Sir Thomas sees Fanny's removal to Portsmouth as 'medicinal'. William looks forward to it as a great thing for his parents and siblings: 'You will tell my mother how it all ought to be, and you will* *be so useful to Susan, and you will teach Betsey, and make the boys love and mind you. How right and comfortable it will all be!' But it isn't—at least for Fanny. Why not?* Because, as she finally realizes, Mansfield Park, not Portsmouth, is her 'home'. She no longer belongs in the station of life into which she was born, except as a missionary bringing (temporarily, we fear) the benefits which William enthuses about. Had Fanny been truly altruistic she might well have dedicated herself, in the long term, to rescuing the Portsmouth Price family from its degradation. But her own destiny is, ultimately, more important. The reader will, in probability, agree with her.

4/25 *Mrs Norris's bitter reflection on the disastrous elopements of the Bertram sisters is: 'Had Fanny accepted Mr Crawford, this could not have happened.' Is she right in her recrimination against Fanny?* Yes. But Mansfield Park would not have been, finally, lodged in the possession of owners best fitted to maintain and live up to it. The 'shock' of his sisters' conduct is a moral education for Tom (susceptible as he is through illness). Improvement is the net result. Particularly if, as seems likely, Fanny and Edmund (Tom being enfeebled) become the eventual owners of the great property.

Emma

Level One

1/1 *The first sentence of* Emma—*as of all Jane Austen's novels—is epigrammatic and memorable. The first epithet ascribed to Emma in it is 'handsome'. What is the overtone of the term?* That she is less than beautiful, that she is self-possessed, that she is more powerful than a mere 'Belle' (like her sister). The first description of Mr Elton is that he is 'a very pretty young man'. How different our initial impression of the heroine would be if the first sentence began: 'Emma Woodhouse, pretty, clever, and rich . . .'

1/2 *How long has Isabella been married? Where does she live, and what do we deduce from these facts?* She has been married seven years and is six years older than Emma. John Knightley, a younger son, could not inherit the Donwell estate so he married early and married rich—the elder Miss Woodhouse, with her thousands in the Consols. The John Knightleys live in Brunswick Square, Bloomsbury, in what is now central London, but which in their day was the northern limit of the capital.

1/3 *What game do Mr Woodhouse and Emma play of an evening, at Hartfield?* Backgammon—a board game which nowadays has suggestions of the sinful casino. They apparently (from later references) play for 'sixpences' when visitors come. The point being made is that theirs is not an evangelical household.

1/4 *How old is Mr Knightley?* He is 37 or 38. Why, one goes on to wonder, has he never married? Either because he is waiting for Emma, or he has had to get his estate in order. It is not excessively far-fetched (if rather un-Austenish) to suspect that Mr Knightley has a respectable lower-class mistress tucked away somewhere; not, obviously, in Donwell, to offend the neighbours; but maybe some innkeeper's wife/widow or similar, whom he visits when he goes to Richmond or Kingston markets.

1/5 *How old is Mr Elton?* 'Six or seven-and-twenty'. He is some three years older than Frank, and twelve years younger than Mr Knightley. Mr Elton would have been ordained for three or four years, and done a first curacy before getting the living of Highbury. He has it, presumably, by virtue of his ingratiating manner, excellent character, and 'pretty' looks: he seems to have no family connections or 'interest' around Highbury.

1/6 *How often does Frank see his father?* Once a year, in London. He did not attend his father's wedding.

1/7 *Who was the widowed Mrs Bates's husband?* The Revd Mr Bates—a former vicar at Highbury. He was not, evidently, the vicar immediately before Mr Elton (who has just taken up the living). Talkative as the Bates household is, they never talk about him.

1/8 *How old is Harriet, what distinguishes her from the other forty pupils at Mrs Goddard's, and who are her parents?* She is 17, a beauty, and 'the natural daughter of somebody' (a somebody in 'trade', as we eventually discover). She has, as the novel opens, been recently raised from 'the condition of scholar [that is, ordinary pupil] to that of parlour-boarder' (that is, she lives, as one of the family, with Mrs Goddard). Harriet evidently knows nothing of her father (nor her mother). Mrs Goddard may (but vouchsafes nothing to Emma). Harriet is, one presumes, not of local origin—otherwise gossip would supply the name of her parents.

1/9 *What colour (precisely) are Emma's eyes?* They are of 'the true hazle' and 'brilliant'.

1/10 *How many children does Isabella have, and what are their names?* Five. In descending order: Henry, John, Bella, George, and baby Emma, aged eight months. She has been married seven years or so. Emma sketched them all two years ago, when there were just the four children. Emma is a fond aunt, we deduce.

1/11 *What do we deduce from the fact that, in twenty-one years,*

Emma has not met the Martin family? The Martins live in the adjoining Donwell village/parish, not Highbury, hence Emma is not likely to see them on a daily basis. And, as she explains to Harriet, they are prosperous farmers, neither poor nor gentry. So on the one hand there is no reason for her to think of them as possible recipients of her charity, and on the other hand she cannot know them as social equals. They, of course, know her by sight.

1/12 *Who did Miss Nash's sister marry (very advantageously)?* A linen-draper.

1/13 *Who is the best whist player in Highbury?* Mr Elton. He is not, we deduce, 'high church'.

1/14 *How large a contingent of servants and cattle does it take to get the five-strong Woodhouse party three-quarters of a mile to Randalls, on Christmas Eve?* Four servants and four horses.

1/15 *What piece of land separates Randalls from Hartfield?* The 'common field', symbolically enough.

1/16 *How long is it since Jane Fairfax was in Highbury?* Two years—about the same time that Mr Elton came and, presumably, the old vicar died.

1/17 *Who was Jane Fairfax's father?* Lieutenant Fairfax, an infantry officer, who married Mrs Bates's youngest daughter. He subsequently died in action abroad. She followed with a consumption.

1/18 *How much money did Miss Campbell bring to her marriage, by way of dowry? And how much are the other eligible ladies in the novel worth?* Miss Campbell brought her lucky husband £12,000. Augusta Hawkins (later Elton) is worth £10,000 and Emma, most desirable of all, £30,000. These sums can be multiplied fifty-fold to reach approximate modern-day values.

1/19 *What is Mr Elton's first name? And Mr Knightley's? And Mrs Weston's? And Mr Woodhouse's?* Philip, George, Anne, Henry.

1/20 *What does Mr Knightley do with his last stored apples of the year?* He gives them to the Bateses—more particularly to the visibly ailing Jane. Vitamin deficiency was known, if not by name, then by the sufferer's pallid complexion (the blemish in Jane which the duplicitous Frank points out to Emma). The apples furnish the only lie we catch Mr Knightley in when he reassures the Bateses he has plenty of the fruit left—something later indignantly contradicted by his steward, William Larkins, who evidently disapproves of Donwell's bounty being given away.

1/21 *With whom did Augusta Hawkins principally reside at Bath?* Mrs Partridge—chaperone and (genteel) boarding-house keeper. The name suggests hunting: not, of course, for game, but marriage partners.

1/22 *What is the name of Mrs Elton's cook?* Wright. Mrs Elton is assiduous in collecting 'receipts' (that is, recipes) for Wright from the Highbury families. She intends to entertain in style. One assumes that when she served the bachelor vicar, life was easier for Wright.

1/23 *Who is whose caro sposo and who is whose caro sposa?* Mr Elton—his wife (or possibly Jane Austen, or possibly some proofreader at John Murray's) is not sure about Italian gender.

1/24 *What is Mrs Weston doing when she breaks the news of Frank's duplicity to Emma?* She is at 'her work'—seven months pregnant, she is sewing in preparation, we may assume, for her soon-to-be-born child. Knitting was considered somewhat low class and would have been less likely for someone of Mrs Weston's station. Specifically, she is sewing her 'broad hems', that is, dresses for the baby with a large turn-up at the hem, so that it can be let down as the child grows. She has also, we learn, made a first set of caps.

1/25 *How long has Mr Knightley been in love with Emma?* 'Since you were thirteen at least'. Presumably he found Isabella too stupid (and like her father) for his taste and let John take her.

Level Two

2/1 *How long has Miss Taylor been in Mr Woodhouse's employ, before becoming Mrs Weston, and what can we deduce from it?* Sixteen years—Emma now being almost 21. She was evidently first taken on as a nursery governess aged, one deduces, 18 or so at the time (if she is nubile and fertile at the beginning of the novel).

2/2 *What does John Knightley do for a living?* He is a lawyer. His large new house in Brunswick Square is close to the Inns of Court. The large house was, presumably, bought with Isabella's money as his partnership will have been.

2/3 *Why did Mr Knightley not go to Miss Taylor's wedding (thinking well of her, as he obviously does)?* He was away from Highbury, and she and Mr Weston were not, presumably, of sufficient 'consequence' for him to put off a trip. Weddings were, anyway, small affairs at this period and a large gathering would not have been expected.

2/4 *How long did Mr Weston court Miss Taylor, and when did Emma contrive to 'make the match'?* It began four years ago, on the occasion of a happy shower of rain (a 'mizzle') in Broadway Lane. Emma was 16 or 17 at the time. Mr Weston gallantly went to get umbrellas from Farmer Mitchell's.

2/5 *Why did Emma not attend Mrs Goddard's 'honest, old-fashioned boarding-school'?* It is an establishment that teaches a lower kind of female 'accomplishment' than will ornament the rich Miss Woodhouse—sewing, cooking, housekeeping skills. Emma has servants to do these for her. Mr Knightley comments, sharply, on Harriet's 'indifferent' education. There are forty children in the school. Mrs Goddard (there was, quite likely, no 'Mr Goddard': 'Mrs' is very probably a courtesy title, awarded by virtue of her age and dignity in the community) at one point says she has 'formerly owed much to Mr Woodhouse's kindness'. We assume he has given a sizeable donation to the school.

2/6 *What do we know of Robert Martin, his practice as a farmer, and his preferred reading?* He is the son of a prematurely dead farmer-father and now, aged only 24, has early in life an opportunity to try out his novel 'improving' theories of agriculture and pastoral farming. Few young men, in the nineteenth century, had their own farm in their early twenties. He reads, for business, the Agricultural Reports and for recreation *The Vicar of Wakefield*.

2/7 *What is Harriet's favourite reading?* Two titles we know about are *The Romance of the Forest* and *The Children of the Abbey*. She is drawn to them because they have foundling hero-ines—like herself, as Harriet fondly thinks. Her taste (fed, one assumes, by Highbury's circulating library) is for the romantic book of the day: Mills and Boon, early nineteenth-century style.

2/8 *Who is Mr Elton's closest male friend in Highbury and who is his most devoted female admirer?* Mr Cole is his closest male friend—one of the first glimpses we have of them is arm-in-arm, confirming manly intimacy (are 'Miss Woodhouse' and Harriet ever arm-in-arm? Probably not). Mr Elton's fondest lady admirer is Miss Nash, head-teacher at Mrs Goddard's little academy. Miss Nash has written down all the clergyman's sermon texts and longingly admires the new yellow curtains at the Vicarage.

2/9 *How many Emmas do we encounter in this novel?* Two. The other is Isabella's youngest daughter.

2/10 *What do 'little Bella' and Harriet Smith have in common?* Sore ('putrid') throats.

2/11 *Does Emma have a personal maid, and what do we know of her?* Yes. We know nothing about this nameless abigail. She is mentioned only once, after Mr Elton's provoking proposal. She curls her mistress's hair before she retires for the night (whether she takes out the curling papers in the morning is not mentioned).

2/12 *What, precisely, do we know of the Woodhouse family and pedigree?* They have been 'settled for several generations at Hartfield, the younger branch of a very ancient family'. Why then, one might wonder, are there no connections with the distinguished major branches? Hartfield has, we understand, 'inconsiderable land'. Where, then, does its grandeur originate? Not in aristocratic connection, land-holding, or vast wealth.

2/13 *Randalls is sometimes said to be three-quarters of a mile from Hartfield, and sometimes half a mile. How does one account for the difference?* It depends whether you cut across the common field or not.

2/14 *'There are men who might not object to—' Harriet's illegitimacy, Mr Elton is about to say. How does he know she is illegitimate?* As vicar, he would have access to all the births, marriages, and deaths inscribed in the parish register. But, of course, Harriet was probably not born in Highbury. It seems to be common knowledge that she is illegitimate but her actual parentage is unknown—on the other hand, if she is not a local girl, there was absolutely no reason for some convenient fiction not to have been concocted, to protect her reputation and prospects in life.

2/15 *Where did Frank and Jane fall in love?* Weymouth. It was Frank, not Mr Dixon, we may deduce, who really saved her from drowning. Of course, like all young ladies of her time, she would not have been able to swim—although a Byronist like him would have been able.

2/16 *What 'trade' may we assume Mr Cole to be in?* Unspecified.

The family, we are told, are 'of low origin, in trade, and only moderately genteel'. They have been neighbours of the Woodhouses for some years and have come into the country after enriching themselves in London.

2/17 *Does Emma seriously suspect adultery, or adulterous intent, among the Weymouth set?* Yes. It is the kind of thing that could happen at a fashionable resort, but never at Highbury.

2/18 *Why does Harriet hate Italian singing?* Because there is 'no understanding a word of it'. It is not clear that even Emma understands it. Jane Fairfax does.

2/19 *Why does Mr Knightley think Jane unattractive as a prospective wife (apart, of course, from her pennilessness and lack of acres)?* She has 'not the open temper which a man could wish for in a wife'. He does not want a partner who keeps anything from him (money, opinions, personal affairs). Is *he* open, one may ask? In his having loved Emma (not as an uncle, but as a prospective suitor) since she was 13? No.

2/20 *What is Jane Fairfax's 'daily errand'?* A walk to the post-office—even in the driving rain. John Knightley, who quizzes her about this chore, seems, astute investigating barrister that he is, to know that something secret is involved. Has he told his brother George? And did Mr Knightley put two and two together?

2/21 *How is the visit to Hartfield by the two little boys Henry and John indirectly responsible for Mr Knightley becoming suspicious of Frank Churchill's behaviour towards both Emma and Jane Fairfax?* Frank Churchill asks Emma: 'have your nephews taken away their alphabets—their box of letters? It used to stand here. . . . We had great amusement with those letters one morning. I want to puzzle you again.' Mr Knightley then notices that Frank's anagrams of 'Dixon', 'blunder', and 'pardon' have some particular meaning for both Emma and Jane.

2/22 *Who, as we are told, 'has always been rather a friend to the* *abolition [of the slave trade]'?* Mr Suckling. The qualifier 'rather' is interesting.

2/23 *Who 'always travels with her own sheets'?* Selina Suckling (née Hawkins), fearful, presumably of damp sheets or any hostelry bedbug.

2/24 *Why, if Selina Hawkins has made such a fine match with the owner of Maple Grove (with a barouche landau, to boot), does her sister Augusta have to make do with a relatively impecunious country clergyman? And why did she marry him so precipitately, without even looking over the living at Highbury where she would, probably, spend the rest of her life?* The contemporary reader, given Mrs Elton's 'prettiness' and her £10,000 dowry, might well suspect some skeleton in her closet—that she is, in some way, damaged goods.

2/25 *What prevents Harriet from running away, when confronted by thieving, dangerous gipsies?* An attack of cramp, consequent on her dancing the night before at the ball. It makes one doubt whether she will make a terribly effective farmer's wife for Robert Martin.

Level Three

3/1 *Where does Mr Woodhouse's great wealth come from?* He has no known relatives (known to the reader, that is). He did not, we are told, marry early in life. Was his money made (hard to imagine) or inherited? He has been, we are told, a 'valetudinarian all his life'—from which we assume he has lived that life in the lap of luxury. Hartfield has been in the family for generations—but there is no land, or farms (other than a field or two), attached to it. No tincture of trade is evident. Oddly, Emma seems to have no maternal or paternal relatives at all. We assume that her mother came from a different part of the country, that Mr Woodhouse was an only child, and that his money has been sanitized by many generations of wealth. The absence of land around Hartfield may, however, suggest that his wealth has come from the sale of arable property—but to whom? Possibly to a predecessor of Mr Knightley, who is the largest landowner in the area. Possibly to Mr Knightley's father. Possibly an addition of wealth came with Emma's mother, of whose family background we know nothing.

3/2 *How old is Emma, and what does her age signify?* She is 'nearly twenty-one'. When she reaches 'long-expected one and twenty' (Johnson) and majority her inheritance will be hers, and a prize for any prospective suitor. Possessed of £30,000, she is a prize worth winning. Emma was 16 when her older sister, Isabella, married—aged 22 or 23. She was, one imagines, possessed of a similar fortune/dowry.

3/3 *How old is Mr Woodhouse?* In his pampered sixties, we deduce. We may further deduce that he must have been some twenty years older than his dead wife, Emma's mother. What, one may go on to ask, ails him—it would seem, self-evidently, that he was once vigorous enough to sire two daughters. Is he perhaps the victim of Alzheimer's disease—something which Jane Austen might well have observed but which medicine had not yet learned how to diagnose?

3/4 *What do we know of Mr Weston and his background?* A lot. He comes from a 'respectable family which for the last two or three generations had been rising into gentility and property' (which implies that the Woodhouse wealth, by contrast, is older than three generations). He has the benefit of a good education and a 'small independence'. He left brothers in 'trade' (what trade?) and bought a commission in the militia (given Frank's age, and the presumable historical setting of the novel, 1814, it must have been in the period before the Revolutionary War). He was posted to (or visited) Yorkshire, where he met 'Miss Churchill, of a great Yorkshire family' (a branch, we may deduce, of the extremely great Marlborough Churchills). Miss Churchill married to disoblige her family—accepting the offer of the militia lieutenant. The Westons had one child, Frank. Three years after marriage, the first Mrs Weston died. Mr Weston, now (mysteriously) impecunious—or perhaps merely unwilling to take on the responsibility of a child—passed Frank on to the childless Mr and Mrs Churchill (his brother- and sister-in-law). They took 'whole charge' of the child. We do not know if they legally adopted him. The fact that he took on their name suggests they did. Mr Weston subsequently sold his commission and quitted the militia, returning to the family 'trade'. This was eighteen or twenty years ago (which would put him, when he marries Miss Taylor, in his mid- to late forties). He has, for some reason, been boycotted utterly by Enscombe—the family seat of the Churchills. He has, however, prospered sufficiently to retire entirely and buy Randalls.

3/5 *What feminine 'beauty' does Emma particularly admire?* That of Harriet Smith. She is 'short, plump and fair, with a fine bloom'. She has blue eyes, regular features, and an expression of great sweetness. The one 'fault' in her face is the lack of good eyebrows. Emma, who draws portraits, has anatomized her physiognomy carefully.

3/6 *Emma mentally divides society into four ranks: the poor, the yeomanry, the gentry, and the nobility. To which group does Robert Martin belong?* In her opinion, the yeomanry—'precisely the order of people with whom I feel I can have nothing to do. A degree or two lower, and a creditable appearance might interest me; I might hope to be useful to their families in some way or other. But a farmer can need none of my help, and is therefore in one sense as much above my notice as in every other he is below it.'

3/7 *Robert Martin, we learn, has an 'unmodulated' voice and has no 'air', such as Mr Knightley has. What do these terms mean?* Presumably that he has a regional accent, and that—farmer that he is—he walks with a somewhat heavy-booted gait (he has never had dancing lessons, as the Knightleys will have had).

3/8 *What do we know of Mr Elton's background?* That he has no 'low connections' (nor, vehemently, does he intend to form any with the 'natural daughter of somebody'). None the less, as Emma evidently knows, his family is not sufficiently 'consequential' to object to Harriet's 'doubtful' birth. There is a taint of 'trade'. Presumably he is the first member of his family to go to university. He has some private means and what we assume to be a fairly good church living.

3/9 *'Men of sense', says Mr Knightley, 'do not want silly wives'. How, then, does he account for his very sensible brother John marrying very silly Isabella?* There is an unstated parenthesis to Knightley's truism: 'unless, of course, they are richly endowed'. Younger sons, as Colonel Fitzwilliam (another sensible man) ruefully observes in *Pride and Prejudice*, may not marry where they will.

3/10 *In conversation when, as Mr Knightley reports, 'there are only men present', Mr Elton has indicated his intentions of setting his hat at the daughters (twenty-thousand pounders, each of them) of a family with whom his sisters are intimate. Why then is he targeting Emma, and has he confided his intentions about Miss Woodhouse to Mr Knightley?* Men are more open with each other in all-male company than when they are in mixed company. Elton realizes that, with an old and ailing father, Emma will one day be worth much more than her current £30,000. And he does not confide in Knightley because he is shrewd enough to perceive the other man as a potential rival.

3/11 *Who lives at Clayton Park?* We don't for a certainty know, although it is mentioned that Mr Perry treats someone there. The Gilberts seem the likeliest candidates. They must, presumably be (even) richer than the Woodhouses although Emma, as far as we know, never visits anyone grander than herself in the environs of Highbury. The residents of the Park are the novel's unglimpsed grandees like those anatomized at length in *Mansfield Park*.

3/12 *How good a vicar is Mr Elton?* He is clever, and the best whist player in Highbury. He has not, we learn, visited the wretched cottagers that Emma and Harriet call on. On the other hand, the young ladies meet him when he is just on his way to do so. Harriet (for whom he can do no wrong) describes him as a friend to the poor. Later, via Mrs Elton, we learn that he has a regular Saturday meeting with Mr Knightley (a magistrate) to discuss matters of relief and workhouse provision. We do not know his theological position—but it seems not to be 'low'. He plays cards and drinks to the brink of drunkenness—on the night before the most sacred day in the Christian calendar, no less, when he should, if devout, be working on his Christmas Day sermon. He shops in Bond Street (for personal jewellery, we presume). He goes off to Bath, where, one assumes, he dances better than the clumsy Revd Mr Collins who makes an ill figure on the floor. On the whole, Mr Elton is a credit to his cloth.

3/13 *Why does Emma dislike Jane Fairfax—a young lady of high education and good breeding, whom she has known since childhood?* Because she is quite simply jealous, as Mr Knightley ruthlessly points out: 'She saw in her the really accomplished young woman, which she wanted to be thought herself.'

3/14 *Desperate to change the subject in the epic Perry versus Wingfield physician controversy, Emma asks John Knightley about his friend Mr Graham bringing in a Scottish bailiff to manage his estate. 'But will it answer?' she asks; 'will not the old prejudice be too strong?' What is the 'old prejudice'?* That still attaching to the Jacobite Scots (memories of Bonnie Prince Charlie's uprising of 1745) among the Hanoverian English middle classes.

3/15 *'She believed he had been drinking too much of Mr Weston's good wine'. It is one of the most famous lines in Austen. Why does not Emma know that Mr Elton has overindulged?* Because he did so after the ladies withdrew from the dinner table.

3/16 *What, by her meaningful maiden name, do we assume*

Mrs Elton's family made their money in? She comes from 'the very heart of Bristol' and—by association with John Hawkins—we assume that her family made their fortune in the slave trade. Later, when Jane Fairfax makes her bitter remark about 'trade in flesh' (thinking of the market for governesses), Mrs Elton says her brother-in-law, Mr Suckling, has always rather been a friend of the abolition which (together with the Sucklings having bought their property Maple Grove some eleven years ago) suggests that the Hawkins fortune was made before Wilberforce's 1807 bill, abolishing the trade in slaves (but not their ownership in the West Indies).

Names are meaningful in *Emma*. Jane Fairfax is no plain Jane, but has a fair face, Mr Knightley is knightly, Frank Churchill is anything but frank, Harriet Smith is a nobody.

3/17 *What was Frank Churchill doing at Weymouth, the previous autumn?* We may presume he was lined up as a suitable prospect for Miss Campbell, before Mr Dixon moved in. The Weymouth subplot (with the plain heiress, the light-hearted Mr Dixon, Frank winning the governess-companion's heart, a near-drowning) can only be guessed. It may be that the Campbells go to Ireland in order to cool things off somewhat.

3/18 *When he takes his farewell from Emma, and seems—standing at the window with his back to her—to be about to divulge something momentous, is Frank about to propose to Miss Woodhouse, or to confess his involvement with Miss Fairfax?* We never know, nor, presumably, does he. Later he self-servingly claims that confession was what he had in mind. Jane is convinced that he is thinking of deserting her for a richer woman—something that provokes (in Jane) a terrible headache. Is Frank tempted to consolidate his fortune by marrying someone who has the money and rank that the governess does not have?

3/19 *Who 'rather preferred an olive'?* Colonel Campbell, when Mrs Dixon was choosing an olive-coloured shawl as a gift for old Mrs Bates.

3/20 *What is the second occasion that gipsies are introduced into the action, the first being the assault on Harriet? What is the third?* Mrs Elton predicts that the Donwell excursion, to scrump strawberries from Mr Knightley's garden, will be 'a sort of gipsy party'. In the last paragraphs of the novel, we learn that gipsies (we assume) have robbed Mrs Weston's turkey coop.

3/21 *There is some discussion of 'Swisserland' in the novel. Would it be possible to go there during the Napoleonic Wars?* The novel is set in 1814, when European travel again became possible for the middle-class young man of Byronic inclination, like Frank.

3/22 *Arrange Mr Woodhouse, Mr Elton, Mr Perry, and Mr George Knightley in ascending order of height.* Mr Woodhouse, Mr Elton, Mr Knightley. Mr Perry, we are told, is the same height as Mr Elton.

3/23 *Who has the management of (inept) Mr Woodhouse's huge wealth?* Mr John Knightley, we assume (who doubtless passes on the necessary information to his brother).

3/24 *Robert Martin can dine with the John Knightleys in London. Why will he never (as the end of the novel prophesies) dine (along with his wife) with the George Knightleys in Highbury?* Because it is Highbury and the proper standards are maintained.

3/25 *If Mrs Goddard knows Harriet's origins (she is the illegitimate daughter of a rich tradesman) why does Harriet herself not know?* Because, we must assume, the tradesman is a local person— possibly even the proprietor of Ford's, Highbury's most thriving commercial establishment.

Level Four

4/1 *Why is Emma so different in temperament from her sister Isabella and her father? Is there no genetic heritage in Austen's* *world—was DNA not a consideration before Crick and Watson discovered it?* Presumably Emma takes after her mother (after whom we may also presume she was named). Mr Knightley (old enough at 38 to have known Mrs Woodhouse) says 'she inherits her mother's talents'. Isabella, seven years the elder sister, inherits her father's less talented personality. Mrs Woodhouse evidently died before the son and heir to the family's sizeable fortune could be produced.

4/2 *What, educationally, has Emma had from her personal tutor, Miss Taylor, that Harriet has not acquired from Mrs Goddard?* It is not clear that Emma can speak foreign languages (she is very spiteful, in her mind, about Mrs Elton's 'caro sposo', and Jane Fairfax's Italian singing). But it seems that Hartfield has a good library (as a girl, as Mr Knightley recalls, she was always drawing up reading lists). But she is not as bookish as, say, Fanny Price. And no bluestocking (a type Austen disliked) as is Mary in *Pride and Prejudice*. Miss Taylor presumably also taught Emma some music and drawing—although these accomplishments may have come from visiting masters, or have been improved by them.

4/3 *Why does Emma particularly dislike Miss Bates—a woman whose 'simplicity and cheerfulness of nature . . . were a recommendation to every body' (except, apparently, Miss Woodhouse)?* Emma does not tolerate fools gladly. But the principal irritant is that Miss Bates has devoted her life (and any marriage prospects) entirely to the care of a very aged and querulous parent. She is Emma's future, incarnate.

4/4 *'I have always thought it a very foolish intimacy,' says Mr Knightley of Emma and Harriet's friendship, during his first quarrel with Emma (about her inducing Harriet to reject Robert Martin). He adds, 'though I have kept my thoughts to myself'. But we recall him saying to Emma's oldest friend (and intimate): 'I do not know what your opinion may be, Mrs Weston . . . of this great intimacy between Emma and Harriet Smith, but I think it a bad thing.' What* *should we make of this contradiction?* Where Emma is concerned, Mr Knightley cannot always keep his self-possession.

4/5 *The John Knightleys come to Hartfield for Christmas, but only stay until the 28th of the month—because John 'must be in town'. Are there any other deducible reasons for the shortness of the stay?* There is obviously a somewhat vexed relationship between Hartfield and Brunswick Square. John and Isabella have named their first-born ('Henry') after his grandfather rather than his father ('John'), in expectation of a legacy, presumably. But John would seem to be doing well as a barrister and finds his father-in-law (and to a lesser extent his wife when she is with her father) difficult. He would seem to be growing in independence—but not entirely.

4/6 *'I will have nothing to do with it,' says Emma firmly, when Harriet asks for advice about how to respond to Robert Martin's letter of proposal. She then dictates her protegée's response. Does Emma know she is lying, or does she deceive herself in these circumstances?* It is difficult to say where deceit and self-deception meet in her character.

4/7 *When Emma asserts it would be a 'degradation' for Harriet to marry Robert Martin, Mr Knightley exclaims: 'A degradation to illegitimacy and ignorance, to be married to a respectable, intelligent gentleman-farmer!' What are the socio-historical implications?* The notion that a farmer can be a 'gentleman' implies a new order is emerging.

4/8 *At one stage, Isabella has four children, later she seems to have five. How do we explain this?* Baby Emma has arrived quite recently. The earlier reference is to a visit two years ago, when there were only four children.

4/9 *What should we make of the Vicarage being 'an old and not very good house'?* It is not a prosperous living although, apparently, there is only one parish in the better part of Highbury. The impoverished condition of the relict of the former Vicar, the Revd Mr Bates, confirms that the living is not particularly well endowed.

4/10 *Emma is 'compassionate' and visits Highbury's poor, to give them some genteel relief. Most of one chapter in this 400-page book is devoted to this worthy activity. Why, as the person of most consequence in her community, does she not do more?* She has no 'romantic expectations' in such matters. There are no Jeanie Deanses in Jane Austen's world, as there are in Walter Scott's.

4/11 *The ostensible reason for Jane's coming to Highbury is to recover from a bad cold (contracted some months since). It is true her mother died of consumption, but what, may we surmise, were Jane's real reasons for not going to Ireland with the Campbell–Dixon party?* To be ready for Frank's coming to make her his bride—or elope with her if the worst transpired and their relationship came to light. She would, one assumes, never consent to become his mistress (would he invite her to? Possibly).

4/12 *We are told that there is not a creature in the world to whom Emma speaks with such 'unreserve' as Mrs Weston (whom she sees 'every day'). Has she confided to her the marital project for Harriet Smith? Is Mrs Weston her accomplice?* No.

4/13 *What is the name of the family who, if they visit Enscombe, will oblige Frank Churchill to forgo his visit to Highbury?* The Braithwaites. We may suspect they are Bunburys (as Oscar Wilde would say)—a convenient fallback if Jane, as seems possible, does not come to Highbury.

4/14 *'Oh, Mrs Churchill,' exclaims Isabella, 'every body knows Mrs Churchill'. Do they? And how?* We never know, but on the edge of the action Mrs Churchill is one of the most potent players in the Highbury drama. It is most likely that gossip about her has emanated, over the years, from Mr Weston (although his remarks, judging by those he makes in the novel proper, will have been very guarded).

4/15 *Why are the Woodhouses 'first in consequence' at Highbury when they have no land, no grand house, no title? Mr Woodhouse is not (like Mr Knightley) a squire or a JP. What, then, is their 'consequence'?* It could be a projection of Emma's own inflated sense of self-worth. But their old money will certainly give them social standing.

4/16 *Where do the Bates ladies (and, presumably, Jane Fairfax) stand in the Highbury hierarchy, and who owns their home?* In Emma's eyes, they are second or third rate. Unnamed 'people in business' own their house.

4/17 *What kind of farmer is Mr Knightley?* His discussions of such matters as the 'common field' and 'drainage' and his admiration for the resourceful Robert Martin make it abundantly clear that the owner of Donwell, and its lands, is an 'improver'. A scientific farmer—unlike Mr Bennet, for example, who seems to have no interest in his many acres. In terms of livestock and crops, we learn that Mr Knightley has a flock of sheep (as does Robert Martin) and that he raises wheat, corn, and turnips (the last, probably, as winter fodder for the sheep). And, of course, the owner of Donwell has apple orchards and strawberry beds, both of which feature directly in the novel.

4/18 *How many characters in Jane Austen do we know to wear spectacles, and what is the only work we ever see Frank Churchill carrying out?* Old Mrs Bates. Mending her spectacles is the only occupation which we see, or hear, Frank engaged in—and that to further his secret engagement with Jane.

4/19 *It is clear from the Donwell picnic that Emma rarely visits the Abbey. Why not?* Mr Knightley does not entertain. The reason is that his household has no hostess: no wife, sister, or aged aunt to attend to the needs of female guests and make them feel chaperoned and secure. For the same reason the unmarried Mr Elton cannot entertain, which is why Mrs Elton is so keen to make up lost ground, with her elegant programme of entertainment, when she arrives in Highbury. For the same reason (no female in his household), Mr Knightley keeps no carriage.

4/20 *What other functions than Frank Churchill's ball take place at the Crown Inn?* Gentlemen have their 'club nights' there at which, we assume, whist is played for small stakes. Officials of the town, like Mr Elton and Mr Knightley, conduct parish and district business there (to do with poor relief, hospital tickets, the workhouse) on Saturday mornings. It is where the post arrives, and the landlord keeps horses for the regional postal service (the post-office is along the street). Mrs Stokes, who prepares the ballroom, is probably his wife.

4/21 *Why does Mrs Weston think so highly of Jane Fairfax?* Because, unlike Emma, she was a good pupil and a credit to whoever taught her. Where, one might go on to ask, did Jane get her clearly superior education? She was brought up and educated (informally adopted, one might say) by the admirable Campbells as their daughter's equal—which is why they are so reluctant to see her going out to work as a governess.

4/22 *What is John Knightley's gruff commendation of Britain's excellent postal service?* It is a government-run agency. According to John Knightley 'The public pays and must be served well.' It seems that, when he has reached the top of the legal slippery pole, John may go into politics—as a Tory. Who is returned for the borough of Highbury is not indicated in the novel. But, as the principal landowner in the area, the constituency will be in Mr (George) Knightley's pocket.

4/23 *Austen previewed, in her mind, the novel as a three-volume affair—each volume having to 'sell itself' to the library subscriber. What are the big events of the respective volumes?* Volume 1, Harriet and Elton, climaxing at Christmas; volume 2, the arrival of Frank

Churchill and Jane Fairfax in Highbury; volume 3, Box Hill, denouement.

4/24 *When Frank instructs Emma to choose a wife for him with the words 'I am in no hurry. Adopt her, educate her', are we to assume that he has seen through her Harriet matchmaking ruse?* Probably, yes; although the remark is also devised to punish Jane. They had a secret quarrel at Donwell the previous day, and Frank's open flirtation with Emma here on Box Hill impels Jane to consider their engagement at an end, hence her decision to take up Mrs Elton's offer of finding her a post as governess. Had Mrs Churchill not died, would Frank ever have married Jane? Probably not. He is too cautious (or selfish) to elope, and not brave enough to confront his aunt.

4/25 *Mr Elton wanted to marry Emma. Does (the Revd) Mr Elton at least marry Emma and Mr Knightley?* Yes. He also marries Harriet and Robert Martin. Jane and Frank will be married in London, one supposes, as her 'beloved home' is with the Campbells. Weddings (as Mr Knightley's unapologetic absence from Miss Taylor's and Mr Weston's ceremony indicates) are low-key affairs in Highbury in the early nineteenth century.

Persuasion

Level One

1/1 *How old is Anne Elliot?* Twenty-seven—a rather more advanced age in the early nineteenth century than it might seem now.

1/2 *What is the dominant element in Sir Walter's character?* 'Vanity was the beginning and the end of Sir Walter Elliot's character' —vanity in the sense of 'egoism' and, secondarily, 'futility' ('vanity of vanities, saith the Preacher': in this case, implieth the novelist).

1/3 *Why is the period (1814) propitious for the letting out of fine country houses like Kellynch Hall? And who duly rents the establishment?* The end of the Napoleonic Wars, certified by the Peace of Paris in June 1814, means that there will be a harvestable crop of 'rich Navy Officers ashore', demobilized, wanting to relax and spend their prize money in leisured, elegant surroundings that they have not been able to assemble themselves, being pre-occupied with the defence of the realm. Peace (after victorious war) is good for real estate. Admiral Croft duly succeeds as occupant of Sir Walter's Somerset seat.

1/4 *How are the Crofts related to the Wentworths?* Mrs Croft, the Admiral's wife, is the elder sister of Frederick Wentworth.

1/5 *What is Mrs Clay's connection with the Elliot family?* She is the widowed daughter of Sir Walter's wily lawyer and agent, Mr Shepherd. Mrs Clay also has her wiles and as 'a clever young woman' has Sir Walter in her sights. Her freckles and worryingly prominent tooth may disadvantage her in his critical eyes; as, to the fastidious Sir Walter, might her 'clumsy wrist' (evident, pre-sumably, when she plays any instrument such as the harp). She will also have to combat the apprehension of Lady Russell and Anne (whose position, with a stepmother her own age, would be impossible). All we know of Mrs Clay's marriage is that it was 'unprosperous' and, luckily for her, brief. We can only speculate what prematurely did for the late and unlamented Mr Clay. The couple had two children, of whom we know nothing more than that they exist.

1/6 *What rank was Lady Russell's departed husband?* 'Only a knight'.

1/7 *What formal schooling has Anne received?* Three years at school in Bath, following her mother's death, when she was 14 and in the way at home. She disliked it. She is the only Austen heroine who has attended school. It is not, one gathers—from the examples of Louisa and Henrietta—a good thing to have been educated away from home (although in their case, it may have contributed to their exuberant self-confidence). Unlike Emma Woodhouse, Anne knew her mother (whom she resembled), loved her, and was—as we guess—psychologically hurt, if not damaged, by the bereavement.

1/8 *What profession was Frederick Wentworth's father?* We never know. His brother was a humble curate at Monkford, 'a nobody', as Sir Walter kindly puts it. The family does not, we suspect, have much in the way of private means. It is true that the Revd Edward Wentworth is now married and has a living in Shropshire, and has made a little way up in the world—but he is clearly only a country cleric, of modest means compared to his nautical brother.

1/9 *Why cannot Anne accompany the Charles Musgroves on their first visit to the Crofts at Kellynch Hall?* Because Charles's curricle only carries two people—one passenger and one to drive.

1/10 *How do Anne and Frederick greet each other, after eight years' separation?* 'A bow, a curtsey'.

1/11 *How many Charleses are there in the novel, and how many Walters?* Children are named as putative heirs. Charles Musgrove is named after his father, and his eldest son, little Charles, is named after him. Charles's second son, Walter, is named after his maternal grandfather, from whom he can reasonably expect a bequest (assuming the vain baronet does not spend all his substance before he dies). Sir Walter's distant heir, William, has Walter as his middle name. There are two other Charleses in the narrative, Charles Hayter and Charles Smith. It creates an occasional confusion.

1/12 *How often has Mary Musgrove been in her relatives', the Hayters', house at Winthrop?* 'Never ... above twice in my life'. Her father's daughter, she despises the connection as 'low'—or, at least, beneath a baronet's youngest child.

1/13 *Has Anne ever visited Lyme before?* Apparently not, judging by the apparent novelty of the tour they all take around the resort, and Anne's later saying to Wentworth 'I should very much like to see Lyme again'. It may seem odd, the coast being so near Kellynch; but the resort was not fashionable (an all-important consideration for Sir Walter). An early nineteenth-century guidebook tactfully recommends Lyme as being suitable for people of limited income: 'a retired spot ... lodgings and boarding at Lyme are not merely reasonable, they are even cheap; amusements for the healthy, and accommodations for the sick, are within the reach of ordinary resources.' Definitely not somewhere for a conceited baronet and his family.

1/14 *What is Lady Russell's favourite recreation?* Like Anne's, reading. She likes books and bookish people. It is something that has gone against both Frederick (man of action) and Charles Musgrove (sportsman) as suitors for her protegée, Anne.

1/15 *What is the 'domestic hurricane' in the Musgrove household?* Christmas festivities, when all the children are home from school. Along with Scott's *Marmion* (1808), the novel offers one

of the fullest literary descriptions of how the holiday was celebrated in the early nineteenth century, before the Victorians made
it what it now is.

1/16 *Bath rings to the bawling of street vendors (such as muffin-men
and milk-men) and the 'ceaseless clink of pattens'? What are these?*
Pattens were wooden soles set upon an iron ring, with straps that
were then tied over the instep of the already-shod foot. This
raised the wearer about an inch above the wet/muddy/messy
road beneath, and hence kept the soft fabric or leather shoes clean
and dry. When first invented it seems all classes wore them; but
then of course it became obvious that any lady would not be
walking in a dirty street, she would be in a carriage; therefore to
wear pattens meant you were lower class. In Bath, at this date,
pattens were probably being worn mostly by tradeswomen,
although a few ladies may have used them just to putter around
local shops. Jane Austen and her sister Cassandra certainly wore
them in the muddy lanes of Steventon and Deane.

1/17 *What does Sir Walter regret in his heir, William's, otherwise
satisfactory appearance?* 'His being very much under-hung'—
that is, having a long lower jaw which projects, unaesthetically,
beyond the upper, giving the face a bulldog-like appearance.

1/18 *How long must Mr William Elliot decently mourn his deceased
wife, before being able to remarry?* About a year, as social arbiters
like Lady Russell assume. In fact, he is prepared to ride roughshod
over such niceties.

1/19 *How big is the blister on Mrs Croft's heel?* 'As large', the
Admiral says, 'as a three shilling piece' (around an inch and a
half). The Crofts in Bath do not believe in wasting their money
on coaches when God gave them legs.

1/20 *What, in Admiral Croft's view, is James Benwick's principal
failing?* He is a little too 'piano'—or soft (his taste for poetry has
done him no good in the profession).

1/21 *What kind of acquaintance does Sir Walter tell the Dalrymples he has with Captain Wentworth?* 'A bowing acquaintance'—he merely knows the gentleman's name, and that he is a gentleman.

1/22 *How old is William Elliot?* Thirty-four, which makes him the oldest lover in the action (unless we include the self-loving, 54-year-old Sir Walter).

1/23 *How much has Captain Wentworth in prize money, to support him in civilian life?* A cool £25,000 (it translates as a seven-figure sum, in modern currency). We discover the sum only late in the novel. As a post-captain, he will get automatic promotion, should he stay in the service.

1/24 *When Captain Harville tells Anne 'if I could but make you comprehend what a man suffers when he takes a last look at his wife and children, and watches the boat he has sent them off in, as long as it is in sight, and then turns away and says, "God knows whether we ever meet again!", ' what, exactly, is he picturing?* The fond father and husband has his wife and family accompany him aboard ship, when embarking on a voyage (which may be for years, and may end in death in battle), before dispatching them back in a liberty boat. It is, in passing, one of the more moving moments in the novel and makes one rather love the bluff sea dog.

1/25 *What is Anne's final good turn in the novel to those less fortunate than her lucky self?* She induces Captain Wentworth to recover Mrs Smith's property in the West Indies, returning that lady to a decent station in life.

Level Two

2/1 *Does Anne take after her mother, or her father?* Her mother, as we are told. It is an important question in Austen's fiction. Emma, for example, takes after her mother. Elizabeth Bennet (fortunately for her) takes after her witty and acerbic father.

Fanny Price seems to take after neither of her parents; lucky for her that she does not.

2/2 *When did Anne and Frederick first become attracted to each other?* During his shore leave, in Somerset, in 1806—the period just after Trafalgar.

2/3 *Could Anne, had she been stronger willed, have married the young Commander Wentworth (as he then was)?* She was, at the time, 19, and would have required parental consent. She could of course have eloped. It is not clear whether Sir Walter, embarrassed as he is for money, had settled anything on her by way of dowry.

2/4 *Who is Sir Walter's favourite and who his least favourite daughter, and why?* Elizabeth, who resembles himself, is his favourite: for her, 'he would really have given up any thing' (there are other suggestions that their relationship is closer than is conventionally that of a father and daughter). Anne ('only Anne') has very inferior value in his eyes. She resembles her mother—the mother who signally failed in her marital duty to supply him with an heir and future baronet.

2/5 *Why should Sir Walter (whose income, when managed by Lady Elliot's good sense, was quite adequate) be 'distressed for money'?* Lifestyle, in a word, or as he puts it, 'Journeys, London, servants, horses, table'. Mr Shepherd astutely realizes that he cannot 'be trusted in London' and dispatches his employer to Bath, where the luxuries of life are cheaper.

2/6 *What naval action do we know Admiral Croft to have been in, and what naval action Captain Wentworth?* Croft was at Trafalgar, with Nelson, and Wentworth at Santo Domingo, a year later, in 1806. To his credit, Admiral Croft, as far as we know, never talks about his war heroics.

2/7 *What are the principal residences at Uppercross?* The Great (or 'Mansion') House, in which the senior Musgroves live; the parsonage (in their gift, presumably); and the handsome farmhouse upgraded into a 'cottage' (that is, a small country house) in which the Charles Musgroves live. Gradations of everything (naval rank, aristocratic rank, seniority of sister) matter in *Persuasion*.

2/8 *What is the only period of her domestic existence when Anne can be said to have been happy?* As we are told, 'excepting one short period of her life, [Anne] had never, since the age of fourteen, never since the loss of her dear mother, known the happiness of being listened to, or encouraged by any just appreciation or real taste'. Equally surprising is that no one, not even Lady Russell, seems to have observed this unhappiness. Technically, then, Anne may be said to have been happy twice in her life: when her fond mother was alive, and during the period of her courtship by Frederick Wentworth.

2/9 *What, precisely, were Dick Musgrove's delinquencies which resulted in his being so happily dead before his twentieth year?* He was, we understand, 'thick-headed', stupid, and selfish. His only education was, briefly, when a midshipman under the command of Frederick. Poor Dick may have been retarded—an embarrassment to his family (although his mother retains some maternal, if misguided, tenderness for his memory). There is no Betsey Trotwood in Austen's world to look after the Mr Dicks of nineteenth-century middle-class England.

2/10 *Why is everyone so alarmed at little Charles Musgrove dislocating his collar-bone?* He is the heir apparent, and will be carefully watched by the family. There is also the worry that he might have permanently injured his back—at this period such mishaps were feared as a source of paralysis and even death.

2/11 *Why is Frederick Wentworth 'lucky' (as Admiral Croft thinks) to get command of the sloop* Asp *when still in his twenties?* Because he has very little 'interest'—that is to say, the patronage of senior officers like Croft. Wentworth is all merit.

2/12 *Who are the best scholars in the novel?* Charles Hayter has a personal library, as befits a clergyman with a study at home. Captain Benwick, a lover of poetry, has a more portable library, suitable for his cramped cabin space. Anne has had the benefit of what books there may be at Kellynch Hall, and the circulating library at Bath: but, presumably, owns few books of her own. One cannot imagine Sir Walter paying the same attention to his books as, for example, Mr Darcy or Mr Bennet do.

2/13 *There is one reference to excrement in Jane Austen's six major novels. Where is it to be found?* The Crofts' gig (with both the Admiral, and his resourceful lady at the reins) contrives not to fall 'into a rut, nor [run] foul of a dung-cart' on the way back from Winthrop. Given the ladies on board (including Anne), it would have been a memorably unpleasant collision.

2/14 *Where is Captain Harville wounded?* As Uncle Toby (similarly disabled) might say, 'at the battle of Lake Erie' (or some other engagement with the Americans since, as we are told, he received his 'severe' wound in 1812). Physically, since there are references to his lameness, we assume it is a fairly serious leg wound which has stopped short of amputation or invalid retirement.

2/15 *Is it the loss of his beloved Fanny Harville which has turned Captain Benwick to poetry and melancholy?* His taste (unlike the Austen heroine's traditional preference for Cowper) is for very recent, 1810 and after, poetry (Scott's *Lady of the Lake*, Byron's tales), so it would seem that this was a deciding factor.

2/16 *Who has the better manners, Captain Harville or Captain Wentworth?* Frederick. None the less, rather confusingly, Harville is 'a perfect gentleman' and 'polished'. He is also, like Wentworth, a tall man. Benwick is the smallest of the three.

2/17 *What causes the years' long rupture between the Dalrymples and the Elliots?* A picayune point of etiquette. Sir Walter, because of a 'dangerous illness', omitted to send a letter of ceremony (that is, condolence) on the death of the late Viscount (this, one gathers, was some fifteen years earlier). Intercourse is restored at Bath, to the Elliots' delight. It is their main connection with 'the nobility' (baronets not aspiring to that ultra-superior class of English society).

2/18 *What is Mrs Smith's connection with Anne, and what is she doing at Bath?* Three years older, as Miss Hamilton, she was— when Anne was at school at Bath (from the age of 14 to 17) a schoolmate and also her comforter in her bereavement at losing her mother—a kind, elder-sister figure (it would seem that Anne did not encounter much kindness at school). She is in Bath to take the waters for a rheumatic condition which has settled in her legs.

2/19 *How long is it since Mrs Smith saw Mr William Elliot, and why does she want Anne to intercede with him, on her behalf?* Three years. The business about her West Indian property, on which (as a trustee, or executor) he is dragging his heels, is why she feels she needs a friend to make her case to him.

2/20 *For how much would William Elliot, as he protests (according to Mrs Smith), sell his baronetcy, were the title saleable?* Fifty pounds, 'arms and motto, name and livery included'.

2/21 *What makes it possible, at last, for Charles Hayter to make a legitimate bid for Henrietta Musgrove?* The acquisition of a rich living (while a young boy grows up into inheriting it) 'only five-and-twenty miles from Uppercross'. Ordination normally happened when the candidate was in his mid-twenties, so there is the prospect of a good income for several years. There are hopes also of something thereafter. Mary Musgrove snobbishly disapproves, but the match is otherwise very fair ('as times go', says Charles Musgrove, thinking of the disruptions produced by the war). At the very least, it gets an expensive daughter off the Musgroves' hands.

2/22 *What finally reconciles Charles Musgrove to his future brother-in-law, the bookish Benwick?* A famous set-to at rat hunting, in which the naval officer plays his slaughterous part as well as the sportive squire.

2/23 *What finally reconciles the snobbish Elizabeth Elliot to Frederick Wentworth?* She 'had been long enough in Bath, to understand the importance of a man of such an air and appearance as his. The past was nothing. The present was that Captain Wentworth would move about well in her drawing-room. The card was pointedly given.'

It is evident that a small tincture of the congenital Elliot snobbery is to be found even in Anne: see, for example, her somewhat snooty comment on Nurse Rooke: 'Women of *that class* [my italics] have great opportunities, and if they are intelligent may be well worth listening to.'

2/24 *What is the ostensible letter Captain Wentworth is penning, as he is actually tumbling out his declaration of undying love to Anne?* He has been charged with getting a miniature of Benwick reset, so that it may be passed on to Louisa. The miniature was originally intended as an engagement gift from him to Fanny Harville, so that she could gaze on her future husband while he was away at sea. She subsequently died while he was sailing back from South Africa. The episode is not entirely clear (why does Wentworth have the commission, which could quite easily be performed by Benwick himself?). But the poignant duty clearly triggers something wildly passionate in Frederick.

2/25 *Does Lady Russell admit, finally, that her 'persuasion' was wrong?* Yes, although not much is made of it, given the fact that two lives were practically ruined: 'There was nothing less for Lady Russell to do, than to admit that she had been pretty completely wrong, and to take up a new set of opinions and of hopes.'

The corrosive qualifier 'pretty' suggests at best a rather grudging concession and it seems she will continue her persuading ways. She has not, that is, undergone any change of character.

Level Three

3/1 *What, in terms of personal attraction, has the 27-year-old Anne Elliot lost?* She was 'a very pretty girl, but her bloom had vanished early'. 'Bloom' is a word which recurs in the novel, alluding apparently to that biologically brief period between a girl's coming out (that is, becoming nubile) and her fading, like a cut flower (usually in her late twenties) and going on the shelf. Anne is on the threshold and the term 'bloom' hangs ambiguously over her during the course of the narrative. She is, we are later told, an 'elegant little woman of seven and twenty, with every beauty excepting bloom'. Whether elegance can compensate for lost bloom is a nice point. Anne, we are told, recovers 'the bloom and freshness of youth' at Lyme Regis, thanks to the resort's 'fine wind which had been blowing on her complexion'. It is, we gather, a temporary colouring, soon to be gone with the wind. None the less, when he sees her at Bath, Sir Walter congratulates her on her improved complexion and hazards that it must be due to the application of Gowland's Lotion. She is on the verge of that age when cosmetics will, of course, have to be resorted to.

3/2 *Who is the heir presumptive of Kellynch Hall, and why did he not, as designed by Sir Walter, marry Elizabeth?* William Walter Elliot (prudently named, it may be noted, after Sir Walter). He chose, having effectively jilted Elizabeth, to unite himself to a 'rich woman of inferior birth'. It is her father's ineffable snobbishness, one assumes, which may have turned him off—that and the fact that Sir Walter's spendthrift ways were dangerously depleting the property which William might expect to inherit.

3/3 *When Elizabeth tells her sister, by way of praise of her father's nobility, that he 'has kept himself single so long for our sakes', what* *does she mean?* That he has not brought into Kellynch Hall a second wife who would displace her (Elizabeth) and take precedence over Anne, and—by producing an heir—cast them into the shadows, or even out of the house altogether. It is not clear that this is the reason for Sir Walter's remaining unmarried. One wonders why, widowed at 42 and 'a very fine man' (not to say a baronet, with progenitive responsibilities to his title), he has never remarried—more so since there is no direct male heir to inherit Kellynch Hall. He has, the narrative informs us, had a couple of rebuffs which he found mortifying. None the less, there would seem to be good dynastic reasons for trying again. His one son, as he has inserted (pompously) in the *Baronetage*, was still-born. Sir Walter Elliot of Kellynch Hall has himself, and that seems enough. Should he become bored with his own company, he has the *Baronetage* to divert him.

3/4 *We are told that Charles Musgrove does 'nothing with much zeal, but sport'. What else can he be said to do?* He waits. Waits, that is, for his father (Charles I) to die and he to come into his inheritance. (In his turn, his son Charles (III) will wait.) His main occupation, such as it is, is to help his father manage the Uppercross estate which he will one day inherit.

3/5 *When Mary Musgrove, justifying her leaving her sick child, says, 'his papa can, and why should not I?', is it to be read as the rationalization of a bad mother, or the argument of a sensible woman?* Almost certainly, given Mary's incurably selfish, lazy, and snobbish character, the first—she is the genetic receptacle of all her father's least lovable characteristics, without even Elizabeth's saving grace of natural grandeur. But given the fact that Charles Musgrove has no occupation in life other than 'sport', modern readers might question whether he might not play the part of house-husband. This, however, would be somewhat unfair, given the customs of the time (by which the tending of sick children was exclusively the task of the mother, aided by nursemaids). In addition to being a beloved son, little Charles is, of course, the heir.

3/6 *When Frederick Wentworth returns, on indefinite shore leave, and tells his sister that any woman 'between fifteen and thirty may have me for the asking', what would she deduce about his state of mind?* Cooped up on a boat for all those years since leaving Kellynch in 1806, he is practically exploding with lust. Also the 'thirty' threshold (although, like 15, hyperbolic) opens a tiny window of hope in the reader's mind for Anne. She has three years left in the marriage market.

3/7 Persuasion *could perhaps be subtitled, like Sheridan's play*, The Rivals. *How much do the various lovers in the narrative know about their rivals?* It is not clear whether Wentworth knows that Charles Hayter has been a long-time suitor for the hand of Henrietta; nor whether Benwick is aware how much Frederick (temporarily) is contemplating marriage with Louisa. Frederick, almost certainly, is unaware of William Elliot's moves on Anne at Bath. On second thoughts, 'Lovers' Impercipience' might be a better subtitle than 'The Rivals'.

3/8 *Does Mary Musgrove know that Charles took her simply because Anne refused him and she (younger, and less beautiful) was next in line (and, for the union of the two estates, a Musgrove–Elliot match was desirable)?* It is hard not to think that in some effusion of irritation Louisa or Henrietta would have blurted this out. A consciousness of being once thought second best would explain Mary's incessant spitefulness to her gentle older sister. It would also explain her manifest pleasure (strange, given her selfish character) when Anne finally marries the very attractive Frederick. Was Anne, one wonders, 'persuaded' (as Louisa thinks) out of accepting Charles? Or was it his manifest vacuity and brawny philistinism that inspired her to reject him? Why, one wonders, would Lady Russell think Mary suitable, and not her favourite, Anne? (Louisa's further surmise that Lady Russell thought Charles 'not learned and bookish enough' is surely something that Anne, in her twenties, could work out for herself). Lady Russell must have made the shrewd judgement that the coarser-grained Mary would 'do' for coarse-grained Charles. It was a 'match'.

3/9 *What injury does Louisa sustain at Lyme Regis?* 'There was no injury but to the head,' the narrative observes, rather spitefully (her head is not Louisa's most winning feature). She evidently slipped, jumping down the steps which lead from the high part of the new Cobb to the lower Cobb paving below, missed Frederick's arms, and banged her skull. It is odd that she has not also damaged the arm which, surely, she would have thrown out to protect herself.

3/10 *What is the Crofts' principal attraction to Anne, as tenants of Kellynch Hall?* That they will be a good example to the parish and will bestow on the poor 'the best attention and relief'. Such considerations, of course, weigh little with Sir Walter and Elizabeth. The implication is that Anne is the most pious member of her family (see, for example, her growing suspicion of William Elliot, on learning that he had displayed 'bad habits . . . Sunday travelling had been a common thing': and her alarmingly sanctimonious comments about the moral lessons to be learned in sickrooms—commonsensically contradicted by Mrs Smith, who knows personally what it is to be chronically sick). This side to Anne's character perhaps explains Jane Austen's comment about the heroine of *Persuasion* 'being almost too good for me'.

3/11 *What changes, of a minor kind, do the Crofts make to Kellynch Hall, to fit it for their habitation?* They mend the laundry door and remove the full-length mirrors from the master bedroom. The implication is that the worthy Crofts put more stress on clean linen than on cosmetic finery.

3/12 *Why does Mary insist on remaining (instead of Anne) with the invalid Louisa, convalescent with the Harvilles, given her general uselessness and proclivity towards hysterics?* There are a number of hints in the narrative that Mary is not averse to putting a little distance between herself and her 'sporting' husband and her unruly children from time to time. It is probably also the case that Mary wants an excuse to stay on longer at Lyme which, although only a small fishing port, is a far more interesting place to reside than Uppercross Cottage.

3/13 *What support does Mrs Smith have, to keep herself genteel?* She seems to have saved a little from her husband's financial wreckage (incurred, largely, through his friendship with William Elliot). Invalid and unable to move freely, she makes 'little thread-cases, pin-cushions and card-racks' which she sells, ostensibly for charitable purposes (although, evidently, she pockets something for herself, from the sale of her 'merchandize', as she frankly calls it). Her intermediary Nurse Rooke puts her in touch with rich targets like Mrs Wallis—'a mere pretty, silly, expensive, fashionable woman'. Mrs Smith is unusual in Jane Austen's fiction in being a middle-class lady who works ('trades').

3/14 *What, in Sir Walter's view, will 'surprise' Westgate Buildings, where Mrs Smith resides, in the old quarter of Bath?* 'The appearance of a carriage drawn up near its pavement', albeit Lady Russell's vehicle, which has 'no honours to distinguish her arms' on its heraldic device. Armigerous families, such as Sir Walter's, had their coats of arms painted on their carriage doors (rather like a noble version of the personalized number plate). Elsewhere in the narrative William Elliot goes unnoticed by his cousins because the panel on his carriage door that would have identified him is covered by a greatcoat casually hanging out of the window above.

3/15 *What, in Anne's analysis, accounts for the union of the bookish Benwick and the very light-headed Louisa?* Two things. 'Situation'—the fact that they are thrown into each other's company in the confined spaces of Lyme. Secondly, Louisa's head injury produces a strange calming effect on her personality—a kind of benign brain damage. By later account, from Charles Musgrove, 'she is altered: there is no running or jumping about, no laughing or dancing; it is quite different. If one happens only to shut the door a little hard, she starts and wriggles like a young dab chick in the water.' She is, evidently, a martyr to nerves. Captain Benwick is obliged to 'whisper' his poetry, in reciting to her. Her taste for poetry is, apparently, a post-accident thing.

3/16 *How is it that Mrs Smith is so 'penetrating' on the subject of Anne's personal situation at Bath—notably her suspicion that her friend is in love?* Mrs Smith does not go into society, but she uses spies and gossip mongers like Nurse Rooke (carrion-consuming bird) very astutely. But on this occasion there is a basic misunderstanding and some cross-purpose. Mrs Smith thinks Anne is yielding to Mr William Elliot's courtship; she doesn't know anything about Anne's secret love for Frederick. Anne thinks for a moment that her secret has been guessed by her friend.

3/17 *Anne, for (an impressed) William Elliot's benefit, translates the words of an Italian song they have been listening to. Where has she learned the language?* She has either taught herself, or was taught the rudiments in her smart Bath school (opera would have been performed in the town). Perhaps, too, Sir Walter engaged a Italian master for her at some time, as he did to teach her music (she is a good piano performer). It is a love song and, quite likely, the cunning and worldly William (who may know the language himself) feigns ignorance so that words of love will fall from Anne's (innocent) lips.

3/18 *What is the one violation of the 'laws of honour' for which the reader can indict Anne Elliot?* Reading William Elliot's despicable letter of 1803 to Charles Smith.

3/19 *What term of address does Anne use towards her father?* 'Sir'. It is not a concession to his snobbery. Other daughters in Jane Austen's fiction address their fathers by this title.

3/20 *Will the several captains (three of them) remain in the naval service, after the narrative reaches its romantic conclusion—professions often lasting longer than love?* Probably yes, on half pay until such time as any of them is offered a command again. It may be a long wait. Benwick, as Admiral Croft notes, has no friends in high places. Harville is not a well man. He does not seem on the way to physical recovery at Lyme. Wentworth is a 'post captain' which means he is on a seniority ladder which, eventually, should yield him high promotion. But peace time postings are boring and will mean long separation from Anne. It is a nice question whether his exuberant energies will be fully occupied by domestic life—he may, like others, run away to sea.

3/21 *What is Mary's ostensible reason, and what may we assume her covert reason, for approving of Anne's marriage to Frederick?* 'It was creditable to have a sister married' and she enjoys the sense of being a matchmaker. Not that there is now any risk, but she may also be recalling that Anne was once preferred to her by Charles, and it is comfortable to think of her disposed of elsewhere.

3/22 *What will happen, we apprehend, to Mr Shepherd?* Sir Walter's solicitor and agent is, putatively, one of the novel's big losers. Clearly, after his wanton daughter has eloped with the villainous William Elliot (and not married him), the lawyer will not be able to continue in Sir Walter's service. He will have lost his principal client. The errant daughter may not, one imagines, expect a warm welcome at Mr Shepherd's house—unless, that is, she traps the future heir into marriage. For a Lady Elliot, fences might be mended.

3/23 *What reason does Captain Wentworth give for not having proposed again to Anne when he returned, 'in the year eight, with a few thousand pounds' and what would have happened had he done so?* His reason for not renewing his suit is, he says, 'I was proud, too proud to ask again'—which seems unlikely. There was, surely, some lingering resentment. Anne gives him to understand that she would have accepted him. She would have been 21 in 1808, and could have married without parental consent. But, one wonders, would she have withstood, as she had not before, the persuasions of Lady Russell? And would a displeased Sir Walter have withheld any dowry—precipitating the kind of 'love in a

cottage' austerity that Admiral Croft recalls with his Sophie in
their early days at Yarmouth?

3/24 *Will Anne and Frederick have children?* They will have to be
fairly quick about it. It is not clear where they will live—perhaps
they will rent Kellynch Hall. More likely, they will find a home
near some major naval port, such as Plymouth or Portsmouth,
where Frederick—who intends to remain in the service—can
keep in touch with his profession. Who knows, he might
encounter a Lieutenant Price of the Marines.

3/25 *What, finally, happens to Elizabeth Elliot?* She seems
destined to live, frozen in her daughter's role, as Sir Walter's
companion and, in a sense, his alter ego, an incarnation of self-
regard. Possibly some offspring of the Dalrymples may offer for
her. Bath gossip, as Austen's narrative goes out of its way to
remind us, regards her as the handsomest (even at 29) of the Elliot
sisters. But her father seems to be the only partner she has chosen.

Level Four

4/1 *Is 'persuasion', as a moral instrument, good or bad?* The
novel seems to be negative on the question. Persuasion is what
others do to you; 'conviction' is what you develop for yourself. In
Mansfield Park, Fanny Price is convinced that it is wrong for her
to marry Henry Crawford and courageously withstands the persuasion which is levelled at her on every front—in Sir Thomas's
case, from a protector more powerful even than Lady Russell.
The case of Anne Elliot is somewhat different. The advice not
to marry a not-very-well-off naval officer, during wartime, in
haste, and very young (Anne is just 20) was good. Think, for
example, of what happened to Miss Frances Ward and her dashing lieutenant of the Marines: twenty years later, he is drunken,
passed over, disabled, and eking out a living on half pay.

4/2 Persuasion *is unusual in not having the rather loose dating frame* *which contains, for example, the opening of* Mansfield Park *('About thirty years ago . . .'). The opening page of* Persuasion *informs us (principally via the family entry in the* Baronetage*) that Sir Walter was born in 1760 and is now 54; that Anne, the 'persuaded' (in 1806) heroine, was born in 1787 and is now 27. Why this chronological precision?* Because, one assumes, Jane Austen wants us to hear the ominous ticking of Anne's biological clock; as, to be fanciful, the author may have felt that time was running out on her—unmarried, 40, and soon to fall fatally ill. Death is a background presence in the novel: five of the principal characters, Sir Walter, Lady Russell, William Elliot, Mrs Smith, and Mrs Clay, are widowed. Captain Benwick, who lost his fiancée the previous June, may be considered among their number.

4/3 *Why does Sir Walter object to sailors and their current popularity as heroes of the war and saviours of their country?* For two reasons. On grounds of vanity he dislikes intensely what sea-breezes do to the complexion which should, ideally, be pale and transparent, not tanned like 'mahogany' (Mary Crawford offers a warning on the same lines to Fanny, during her sojourn at Portsmouth, about 'sea-breezes'). Exposure to the elements 'ages a man'. And on the grounds of snobbery, Sir Walter objects that since naval service is open to talent, it is 'the means of bringing persons of obscure birth into undue distinction, and raising men to honours which their fathers and grandfathers never dreamt of'. This, of course, is exactly the situation of Frederick Wentworth, the brother of a curate, hugely enriched, at the age of 31, with £25,000 and, as a post-captain, with the prospect being promoted admiral before he is 50. His early promotion, one assumes, is the consequence of merit, not interest. As a post-captain, his later promotion will be a simple question of seniority. Should there be more naval action at sea and he acquits himself as well again, who knows but a baronetcy may even lie ahead of him. In this novel, Austen confronts (as nowhere else in her fiction) the class-turbulence precipitated by war and issues of social mobility.

4/4 *In Jane Austen's fiction, married women often have what we*

would see as psychiatric disorders—vide *Lady Bertram's 'indolence'*
and Mrs Bennet's 'nerves', Mrs Norris's kleptomania. What, if any-
thing, should we read into Mary Musgrove's chronic hypochondria?
She is terminally bored and depressed with the husband whom
Anne, very wisely, rejected. She was, of course, 'taken' only as
second best. 'Even in her bloom', we are told, she was no beauty
(unlike her sisters), and had 'only reached the dignity of being "a
fine girl" '. As a girl no longer, what has she left?

4/5 *There is a long rhapsody, by Frederick Wentworth, on his first*
command, the Asp. *It is the first occasion in the novel on which he may*
be said to be eloquent. What about the Asp *particularly recommends*
it? It is a 'dear old *Asp*', an 'old thing'. It bodes well for the
similarly antique Anne. Old women, like old vessels, have charms.
The name of the *Asp*, with its association with Cleopatra,
reminds us of another heroine whose salad days have passed.
Anne has a similarly meaningful musing on 'autumn' a few pages
later. On a November walk around the Charles Musgroves'
grounds, her pleasure arises 'from the view of the last smiles of
the year upon the tawny leaves and withered hedges'. She, too,
may be seen as a last rose of summer.

4/6 *Why does Frederick Wentworth, a gallant sailor who has been*
under fire, seen men killed alongside him, and taken French ships in
battle, behave like a helpless girl when Louisa falls and bangs her
head, jumping from the Cobb? 'The horror of that moment to
all who stood around!', the narrative breathlessly comments
(among those standing around are two active service, wartime,
naval captains). Wentworth's reaction is histrionic, kneeling by
the fallen lady, 'with a face as pallid as her own . . . "Is there no
one to help me?" were the first words which burst from [him], in
a tone of despair, and as if all his own strength were gone.' It is
Anne who takes charge and calls for a surgeon. One has to assume
that petticoats unman Frederick. Perhaps it is natural modesty—
clearly Louisa's stays will have to be loosened, her wrists chafed,
the omnipresent smelling salts applied to her nostrils. This is not
the kind of action he has been trained for.

4/7 *Lady Russell does not catch sight of Frederick Wentworth all the months he is visiting and staying at Kellynch Hall. She and Anne come across him (Lady Russell for the first time since 1806) in Pulteney Street. Does Lady Russell recognize him then?* Anne is petrified that she will do, but Lady Russell claims that her fixed gaze, in Wentworth's direction, was merely to seek out some window curtains 'which Lady Alicia and Mrs Frankland were telling me of last night'. We may suspect it is perhaps generosity on her part, not to wound Anne's feelings (as she expects) by pointing out the man whom she was induced (by her companion) to turn down, all those years ago. A tactful white lie. Or it could be that she was genuinely on the lookout for curtains. She left for Bath before Captain Wentworth arrived at Kellynch, so she may not recognize him after all these years. Were she more alert, she might, perhaps, notice how perturbed Anne is.

4/8 *Overheard conversation plays a major part in the plot of Persuasion. Anne, for example, happens by chance to be behind a hedge and hears Frederick lecture Louisa, at great length, on the moral quality of the hazel nut. What, relevant to Anne's personal attractions, is accidentally overheard about her at Molland's shop in Bath?* That she is 'pretty . . . very pretty'. But the men of the town 'are all wild after Miss [Elizabeth] Elliot. Anne is too delicate for them.' At this point, Anne has already left Mollands on the arm of the attentive Mr William Elliot. Captain Wentworth overhears the backhanded compliment which, presumably, inflames his jealousy and growing love for Anne.

4/9 *What are Mrs Smith's motives in renewing, so intensely, her friendship with Anne and how do her motives change as the friendship is renewed?* Initially, having learned (presumably from the omnicompetent Nurse Rooke) that there may be romance between Mr Elliot and Anne, she hopes to work on her friend to work on him to negotiate the return of her West Indian property (which, presumably, he is currently profiting from financially). Then, as the friendship deepens, she feels obliged—at the cost of her own hopes—to enlighten Anne as to the true nature of the villain.

4/10 *What can the reader put together of William Elliot's back story?* Most of it comes from Mrs Smith's possibly tainted confidences to Anne. The young Elliot was reading for the law and had chambers in the Temple when he became friendly with Mr Smith. Presumably, he too was a lawyer. Elliot was poor at this stage of his life. It was 'as much as he could do to support the appearance of a gentleman'. At this point, it would have been expected that Sir Walter, producing children with little difficulty, would have a direct male heir. With the death of Lady Elliot, and no male heir surviving, William's prospects improved and he would have been able to raise money on his expectations. His manner of living became more luxurious (and, doubtless, he became more indebted). Always calculating and selfish, he devised a plan to assure his inheritance by marrying Elizabeth but—quite reasonably, we may imagine— he found Sir Walter's company intolerable. The baronet (self-obsessed by nature, wholly unemployed, and very careful about his creature comforts) was likely to be inconveniently long-lived and was, moreover, so extravagant that he was likely to outlive his means, leaving nothing but debts for his heir. William wanted money immediately and married a rich woman whose father (horrible to say) had been a grazier and grandfather a butcher. Huge fortunes were to be made in the provision of meat to the armed forces during the Napoleonic Wars—and William Elliot carved off his share. Mrs Smith's violent remark that he is 'black at heart, hollow and black!' suggests that he may even have seduced, or attempted seduction on, his best friend's wife. There seems more implied than mere meanness or greed.

4/11 *Why does Mrs Smith keep the letter of William Elliot's to Charles Smith, of July 1803, in which he is so coarsely rude about Sir Walter and Miss Elliot and so frank about his mercenary motives?* Quite clearly, if forced to, Mrs Smith will use it for blackmail—should all else fail in prising Elliot away from the West Indian property (her property) that he is holding on to so tenaciously.

4/12 *What does William Elliot protest, in his letter to Charles Smith, will be the purpose of his first visit to Kellynch Hall as the new baronet?* He will go with a surveyor, 'to tell me how to bring it with best advantage to the hammer'. This intention to sell up the ancestral property, a century or more in the possession of the family, and William's other protestation that he would sell the baronetcy, were it saleable, make clear that he is nothing but a Jacobin—a Revolutionary sympathizer. It was not a political opinion much liked by Jane Austen. It would seem that Kellynch Hall and its estate dates from the creation of the baronetcy (which has descended to Sir Walter) in Charles II's reign, the family being 'first settled in Cheshire'. It is pertinent, perhaps, that the Elliots have their title by virtue of loyalty rather than gallantry in the Civil War. It is noticeable that between 1803 (when he confided to Charles Smith his vandalistic intentions) and 1814, William Elliot has changed his tune. He now covets the title, and everything, presumably, that goes with it.

4/13 *What puts it impulsively into Wentworth's mind to write a love letter so late in the day? Why is the letter to Anne so passionate and tumultuous?* The key, perhaps, is the concurrent conversation between Mrs Musgrove and Mrs Croft about 'long engagements' (overheard, as usual, by the bat-eared Anne). There are a number of hints (delicate; necessarily so, given this author) that eight years of enforced celibacy has induced something like rampant lust in Wentworth (see his remark about any woman between 15 and 30 being able to have him). The letter to Anne is an explosion (an ejaculation, one might say) of pent-up desire. He must have her.

4/14 *One of the questions raised, tantalizingly, at the conclusion of the novel, in the conversation between Harville and Anne (as Wentworth, in another part of the room, is writing his love letter), is whether man or woman loves most faithfully. Who has the better of the argument?* It is nicely balanced. Against a background of Benwick's remembered fickleness to his dead sister ('Poor Fanny! She would not have forgotten him so soon!') Harville argues that the stronger sex loves more strongly than does the weaker sex, 'I believe in a true analogy between our bodily frames and our mental; and that as our bodies are strongest, so are our feelings; capable of bearing most rough usage, and riding out the heaviest weather.' To which Anne smartly replies, 'Man is more robust than woman, but he is not longer-lived'. Women may be less libidinous, but are more enduringly and unwaveringly faithful. The line of argument which Harville cunningly introduces (and the veiled confession he elicits from Anne) convince one that he is in Wentworth's confidence, may even know what his ship-mate is currently intending, and is giving it the fairest wind he can.

4/15 *What should one make of Anne's retort to Harville's remarks about the universality, in literature, of the refrain that woman is constitutionally inconstant: 'Men have had every advantage of us in telling their own story'?* Anne—more articulate at this stage of the novel than formerly—does not deny Harville's observation, but goes on to make a subtle point: 'Education has been theirs in so much higher a degree; the pen has been in their hands.' It is significant that she uses the past tense—'has been', with the implication 'up to now'. Redress is, we understand, in order.

4/16 *Is it a failure of invention, or perhaps a mark of exhaustion, that Jane Austen cannot devise some means by which Kellynch Hall should revert to its 'true' custodian, Anne Elliot (as, we assume, Mansfield Park will one day revert to the Edmund Bertrams)?* It could be neither, but rather a refusal to supply a saccharine ending to a consistently tart-flavoured narrative.

4/17 *The first report which Anne hears Wentworth has made about her, after eight years' separation, is that she is 'so altered he should not have known her again'. Yet, in their final reconciliation, he protests, 'to my eye you could never alter'. Is he mis-speaking?* Anne, charitably, assumes that it was 'the result, not the cause of a revival of his warm attachment': that is, his eyes now see things differently from earlier. It is also possible that the revival of erotic feeling and hope in Anne, together with travel and sea air, have improved her appearance—recovered her youthful 'bloom', even.

4/18 *We learn, in the last pages, that William Elliot has been playing a very cunning double game. What is that game, and why is he playing it?* He seduces and elopes with Mrs Clay to remove her from Sir Walter's orbit and any possibility of her pipping him to the post by marrying the baronet and supplying the male heir who will displace him. It seems, for someone credited with Satanic wiliness, the clumsiest of schemes. There is nothing to prevent Sir Walter from looking elsewhere; there are many other fish in the sea (many other eligible ladies at Bath, particularly; ladies without freckles, a protruding tooth, and a background in trade). Why Mrs Clay succumbs is similarly strange—'affection' (that is, carnal lust), not 'interest', we understand; although, as William's concubine, she has a distant chance of becoming Lady Elliot; a better chance, perhaps, than if she had continued angling for the ineffably vain Sir Walter. Objectively, the disposal of William Elliot and Mrs Clay is one of the weaker links in the plot.

4/19 *How did William Elliot 'ruin' Charles Smith?* This is another unconvincing line of subplot in the novel. According to Mrs Smith, Elliot methodically and maliciously 'led his friend into expenses much beyond his fortune'. What, then, was Mrs Smith doing all this while? Could she not restrain her ductile spouse from self-destructive extravagance? It seems more likely, if more melodramatic, that Elliot led Smith into gambling, drink, and sexual dissipation. However 'easy' the late Mr Smith's character, it is hard to think of him being villainously played on by Elliot in the way that his widow describes to Anne.

4/20 *What are we to make of the final sentences about the elopement of William Elliot and Mrs Clay: 'She has abilities, however, as well as affections; and it is now a doubtful point whether his cunning, or hers, may finally carry the day; whether, after preventing her from being the wife of Sir Walter, he may not be wheedled and caressed at last into making her the wife of Sir William'?* The narrative is teasingly open to future developments. Clearly, having advertised her to the world, Mr Elliot has a moral obligation (not that morals mean much to him) to make her an honest woman (again). The break into present tense is interesting, leaving the ending suspended. William Elliot, the coldest-hearted of men, is unlikely, we may feel, to succumb to the caresses of a mere strumpet, caresses which he enjoys without benefit of matrimony anyway. But she is a formidable woman. Another novel lurks here, for a hand less reticent than Jane Austen's.

4/21 *Mary's gratification at Anne's being finally married is, we are told, slightly marred by her 'seeing Anne restored to the rights of seniority, and the mistress of a very pretty landaulette'. What may we read into these details?* Anne, as the older sister and now married, will take precedence at social gatherings (that is, go into dinner before Mary). The 'landaulette' is a two-passenger vehicle, and brisk. There are, we apprehend, no children; and none expected. The stylishness of the vehicle implies that the Wentworths will cut a rather more glamorous dash than the stodgily rural Musgroves.

4/22 *Is 'war', as the novel presents it, a good thing?* War is not good in that it separates men and women so cruelly (as Harville and Croft both testify). But it has the inestimable advantage of allowing talented and courageous sailors like Wentworth—lacking 'interest', inherited rank, or great wealth—to rise to the top of their profession. Had Napoleon not threatened, Frederick would never have been in a position, finally, to claim his Anne.

4/23 *What, in the foreseeable future, will happen to Kellynch Hall?* Oddly, given the huge importance attached to Mansfield Park in the previous novel, *Persuasion* seems strangely indifferent to the fate of the property and lands which Anne so loves. She is, for example, offended even by the thought of the Crofts inhabiting a house which has been in the family since the seventeenth century and, as Lady Russell astutely appreciates, flinches from visiting while tenants occupy it. Assuming that Sir Walter does not marry and produce an heir, William Elliot (wholly undeserving) will inherit and, perhaps, as he threatened to Charles Smith, sell up the property.

4/24 *Are we to assume that Anne will be—in future years—another Mrs Admiral Croft?* It seems unlikely. The description of Mrs Croft suggests a physique very different from Anne's delicate frame and 'blooming' complexion: 'Mrs Croft, though neither tall nor fat, had a squareness, uprightness, and vigour of form, which gave importance to her person. She had bright dark eyes, good teeth, and altogether an agreeable face; though her reddened and weather-beaten complexion, the consequence of her being almost as much at sea as her husband, made her seem to have lived some years longer in the world than her real eight and thirty.' She has not followed her husband into battle, but to various naval stations across the world. Anne is surely incapable of such hardship.

4/25 *Jane Austen's aphorisms are famous and often richly ironic. What can one read into the last sentence of* Persuasion? With the heroine a senior naval officer's wife, and affairs with France unsettled, the end of the novel is overhung with 'the dread of a future war'. Anne is prepared. Unlike its predecessors, *Persuasion* finishes not with stable prediction of a 'settled' condition of life, but radical uncertainty. Uncertainty, even, about the future of the country.

*The
Oxford
World's
Classics
Website*

www.worldsclassics.co.uk

- Browse the full range of Oxford
  World's Classics online

- Sign up for our monthly e-alert to
  receive information on new titles

- Read extracts from the Introductions

- Listen to our editors and translators
  talk about the world's greatest literature
  with our Oxford World's Classics audio
  guides

- Join the conversation, follow us on
  Twitter at OWC_Oxford

- Teachers and lecturers can order
  inspection copies quickly and simply
  via our website

www.worldsclassics.co.uk